# The Biblical Mandate for Believers to Love and Pray for the Jewish People and the Land of Israel

Written to every Christian, Pastor, Leader, and follower of Messiah as a resource for Personal Spiritual Growth and for Small Groups.

## By Kenneth S. Albin

# Introduction

I want to thank you in advance for allowing me the privilege to join you in this journey through the Scriptures concerning the Biblical Mandate to Pray and Love the Jewish People and the Land of Israel. Although we are living in a time when believing Christians are being swayed away from what the Bible clearly teaches, I believe another Great Awakening is happening with people like you and me.

As we embark on this journey of faith, I want you to keep your heart open to learning or, like I say, relearning some things that have been etched into many of us from even before our personal encounter with the Lord. Sometimes the mindset and understanding we have learned or become accustomed to becomes a stumbling block and keeps us from a new or renewed understanding of spiritual truths. If you don't see or understand something right away, don't discount the possibility of it being right or correct. The Hebrew mindset is about doing and then understanding, while the Greek is just about the attaining of more knowledge. The application is much more important as you see in the book of James, which reminds believers to "be a doer of the Word, and not hearers only, deceiving your own selves" (James 1:22).

Since I grew up as a Jew myself, I did not realize until very late in life that the spiritual heritage of every Jew, even if they are secular and non-believing, is rich and majestic in its connection to God, one another and to the Nations in which they might live. I did not appreciate my heritage, even after my own salvation experience, and I tried to hide it. When I became a Christian pastor, I seldom mentioned my heritage or taught about anything about it. I still remember a woman who asked me to teach a small group of her peers about

Passover at the motel she owned in Hollywood Beach, Florida. I studied up a little on the subject and proceeded to share about it in an outdoor setting. At the time I didn't know anything about what I will share in this book. The only thing I definitely remember from that day is, that from the moment I started sharing on Passover, the Holy Spirit kissed that time with a very powerful presence and what I can only call an "anointing" that came over all those who were participating. For some reason that woman, Virginia Swan, had a "love for Israel" and for the heritage that the Jewish people had brought to her through her Messiah. Although she has crossed over into glory many years ago, the memory of that day has been ingrained in my mind and heart.

I learned many years after that experience that the Bible is seamless from the Old to the New Testament. There are threads that connect virtually every story and passage and the promises given to Abraham the Hebrew are just as potent and relevant as they were in his day. Although many have wanted to disconnect the Old and the New because of wrong teaching or misunderstanding, the truth is they are two sides of the same coin. The Old Testament is the New Testament Concealed, and the New Testament is the Old Testament Revealed. They are not contrary to one another and the more you put on the correct spiritual lenses to discern and see correctly, the more life you find in their union.

I have chosen to use a great amount of Scripture in this book, and will do my best to help you see the light of these verses in the correct context and their true and correct meanings, whether it is a Hebrew or Greek text. If you enjoy or learn from this study as a pastor, leader, Christ-follower or if you are part of a group study, please share this resource with someone you think might benefit from this teaching. We know the Bible says that "Light overcomes darkness, and darkness cannot extinguish it." (John 1:5) Let your light shine so all may see the Living One and His love manifest in and through you, all for Messiah's glory! Now let's begin!

# Table of Contents

Chapter One: It's All About the "First Mentions"

Chapter Two: The Million Dollar Question – Who are These "Jews" and what Makes Them so Special?

Chapter Three: Why Should Every Believer Pray for, Seek to Bless and Love the Jewish People?

Chapter Four: The Fig Tree and the Watchmen

Chapter Five: The Fulness of the Nations Is Coming!

Chapter Six: Tying it All Together

Chapter Seven: The Kingdom Way to Pray!

# Chapter One
## It's All About the "First Mentions"

There is something I have been teaching my congregation for quite a while now. It is called the "Law of First Mention." When a word is mentioned the very first time in the Bible, it usually gives you both a context and some type of understanding for what that word will mean as you follow that word throughout the Bible. At times the second mention will also give you this truest understanding as well. In this chapter let's look in the Bible for the first mention of the Land of Israel, as well as the Hebrew word for "Jew." When we look at these very first mentions, we will look at the context and also try to mine or dig out what the Bible is wanting us to discover and understand about them.

We want to first look at the Land of Israel, for it is a very controversial subject in light of the recent war that began in Gaza and has spread to Iran, Lebanon and beyond. Here is the first mention I found.

**Genesis 12:1-3** (TLV) 1 Then *Adonai* said to Abram, "Get going out from your land, and from your relatives, and from your father's house, to the land that I will show you. 2 My heart's desire is to make you into a great nation, to bless you, to make your name great so that you may be a blessing. 3 My desire is to bless those who bless you, but whoever curses you I will curse, and in you all the families of the earth will be blessed.

Notice the phrase **"to the land that I will show you."** This is the first mention of the land promised to the patriarch Abram because he was willing to leave the land of his relatives and his father Terah's homeland.

Strong's Reference for the Hebrew word for **land**:

**H776** אֶרֶץ 'erets, eh'-rets; from an unused root probably meaning to be firm; the earth (at large, or partitively a land): —x common, country, earth, field, ground, land, x nations, way, + wilderness, world.

**Genesis 13:7** (TLV) And there was a strife between the herdsmen of Abram's cattle and the herdsmen of Lot's cattle: and the Canaanite and the Perizzite dwelled then in the **land**.

After God's promise to Abram, he began to go wherever God would lead him. Every place the Lord told him to go, he would build an altar in God's Name. He never built his own city or his own name. He simply, by faith, left the familiar and natural to follow God into the extraordinary and supernatural. Now look what God tells Abram after he separates from his family member Lot because of strife between their herdsman for all their great possessions. Notice that the Bible goes out of its way to insert something right after the "strife." It says that the Canaanite and the Perizzite "dwelled then in the land" of Promise. The descendants of Noah's son Ham were the Canaanites and the Perizzites, among the many other "ite" peoples. They are famous for their trafficking and merchandising which is the meaning behind the Hebrew word for Canaanite. The Perizzite in the Hebrew means belonging to a village. They did not want any outsiders influencing the status quo of those who lived in their little world. The amount of strife in the Land even today can be traced back the spiritual DNA of the people who dwelled alongside of Abram in the Land of Promise. It seems that even today the "Land" is being looked at as "merchandise" and those who live in the Land do not agree on what or if there should be any "changes."

**Genesis 13:14-18** (TLV) 14 After Lot separated himself from him, *Adonai* had said to Abram, "lift up your eyes, now, and look from the place where you are, to the north, south, east and west. 15 For all the land that you are looking at, I will give to you and to your seed forever. 16 I will make your seed like the dust of the earth so that if one could count the dust of the earth, then your seed could also be counted. 17 Get up! Walk about the land through its length and width —for I will give it to you." 18 So Abram moved his tent from place to place, and came and dwelt by Mamre's large trees, which are in Hebron, and there built an altar to *Adonai*.

God told Abram to "lift his eyes." This is a way Biblical Hebrew is hinting to us that Abram was to have spiritual vision in looking at the Land. If you ever have been to the Land of Israel, in the natural it is not so beautiful with all its rocks and desert places. When you go to Israel you have to "lift your eyes" like Abram and see into the supernatural spirit realm to know you are looking at God's Land of Blessings. It has a spiritual beauty and presence like no other place on earth. Abram was told by God that "all the land you are looking at, I will give to you and to your seed (or descendants) forever." He told Abram not only to "lift his eyes," but to "walk about the land through its length the width." In this passage, God also told him with a confirming word a second time, "I will give it to you."

So, through this Law of First Mention we can see the Land of Promise was given directly by God to Abram and his descendants. Abram is a Hebrew, not a Jew, at least not by the typical definition. Abram precedes the Jew because he is the father of all of them, and not just the Jews, but according to the Bible in Galatians, he is the father of all who believe in the Messiah. The Believers in Messiah, according to Scripture, are grafted into the faith of Abraham and become the "heirs according to the promise" with him. Although they are not necessarily native-born Israelites and they can't trace their natural bloodline to Abraham, they do carry the spiritual DNA and, by that right, have been granted to be connected to the commonwealth of Israel.

**Galatians 3:29** (TLV) And if you belong to Messiah, then you are Abraham's seed—heirs according to the promise.

What a blessing and privilege every Believer has to be connected to Abraham and the Land that was promised to his descendants, whether natural or spiritual.

After Abram separated from Lot, he spent a short time in Egypt. and when he came home, he found out Lot had been taken captive in a war of kings and kingdoms. After rescuing Lot and giving a tithe of all to the Priest of Righteousness, Melchizedek, God comes to Abram again, changes his name to Abraham, and confirms this "Promised Land" again and again!

**Genesis 15:1-21** (TLV) After these things the word of *Adonai* came to Abram in a vision saying, "Do not fear, Abram. I am your shield, your very great reward." 2 But Abram said, "My Lord *Adonai*, what will You give me, since I am living without children, and the heir of my household is Eliezer of Damascus?" 3 Then Abram said, "Look! You have given me no seed, so a house-born servant is my heir." 4 Then behold, the word of *Adonai* came to him saying, "This one will not be your heir, but in fact, one who will come from your own body will be your heir. 5 He took him outside and said, "Look up now, at the sky, and count the stars—if you are able to count them." Then He said to him, "So shall your seed be." 6 Then he believed in *Adonai* and He reckoned it to him as righteousness. 7 Then He said to him, "I am *Adonai* who brought you out from Ur of the Chaldeans, in

order to give you this land to inherit it." 8 So he said, "My Lord *Adonai*, how will I know that I will inherit it?"9 Then He said to him, "Bring Me a three year old young cow, a three year old she-goat, a three year old ram, a turtle-dove and a young bird."10 So he brought all these to Him and cut them in half, and put each piece opposite the other; but he did not cut the birds. 11 Then birds of prey came down upon the carcasses, but Abram drove them away. 12 When the sun was about to set and a deep sleep fell on Abram, behold, terror of great darkness was falling upon him!
13 Then He said to Abram, "Know for certain that your seed will be strangers in a land that is not theirs, and they will be enslaved and oppressed 400 years. 14 But I am going to judge the nation that they will serve. Afterward they will go out with many possessions. 15 But you, you will come to your fathers in peace. You will be buried at a good old age. 16 Then in the fourth generation they will return here—for the iniquity of the Amorites is not yet complete." 17 When the sun set and it became dark, behold, there was a smoking oven and a fiery torch that passed between these pieces.18 On that day *Adonai* cut a covenant with Abram, saying, "I give this land to your seed, from the river of Egypt to the great river, the Euphrates River: 19 the Kenite, the Kenizzites, the Kadmonites, 20 the Hittites, the Perizzites, the Raphaites, 21 the Amorites, the Canaanites, the Girgashites, and the Jebusites."

I think by now you have to agree that the Land of Promise was given to Abraham and to his seed by God as a part of a covenant. A covenant is the strongest agreement we have here on the earth and it is absolutely binding, even in the Courts of Heaven. The Land of Israel, of course, does not have this name because it is simply called "the Land." Let me give you a few more biblical proofs as to why it is so important that every Bible believer knows that the Land of Israel is forever deeded to the people that now call themselves Jews or Israel.

The Hebrew word used for the "giving of the land" is a word that points to a gift of grace.

**Give:** נָתַן nâthan, naw-than'; a primitive root; to give, used with greatest latitude of application (put, make, etc.):—add, apply, appoint, ascribe, assign, × avenge, × be (healed), bestow, bring (forth, hither), cast, cause, charge, come, commit, consider, count, cry, deliver (up), direct, distribute, do, × doubtless, × without fail, fasten, frame, × get, give (forth, over, up), grant, hang (up), × have, × indeed, lay (unto charge, up), (give) leave, lend, let (out), lie, lift up, make, O that, occupy, offer, ordain, pay, perform, place, pour, print, × pull, put (forth), recompense, render, requite, restore, send (out), set (forth), shew, shoot forth (up), sing, slander, strike, (sub-) mit, suffer, × surely, × take, thrust, trade, turn, utter, weep, willingly, withdraw, would (to) God, yield.

If you break up the three Hebrew letters and make them into an acronym, it is an undeniable hinting to the gift of the Land of Promise to Abraham.

נ (Nun) the Nun has the numerical value of 50 and it is the 14th letter of the Hebrew alphabet a number pointing to Messiah. This letter is associated with faithfulness and its reward. The number 50 points to Jubilee and the 50 days of waiting to receive the Torah and the Holy Spirit on Shavuot-Pentecost.

ת (Tav) the numerical value of 400 and means to "mark" or "seal". The Tav is the final letter of the Hebrew alphabet. Yeshua called himself the "Aleph and the Tav" in the book of Revelation. When a person puts their faith in the God of Israel, they are marked by Him and receive the seal of the

Holy Spirit as an earnest of the World to Come. The number 400 is 10 times 40. 40 is the number for the completion of a test or time of testing like Israel in the desert for 40 years or Yeshua in the desert being tested by Satan for 40 days. After the testing comes the seal or mark of identification of belonging to the Lord. In ancient Hebrew, the Tav looked much like a cross.

ן (Final Nun) The final or Nun Soffit (appearing in this form at the end of a word), is a completion of the work of the nun. In the Hebrew, the word "nun" means fish or posterity. This confirms the gift of the Land to Abraham's descendants who are blessed to multiply like fish in the land (Genesis 48:16). The root word for nun means "to continue, to propagate and to continue and increase by shoots." The first and last letter of the Hebrew word for "give" are both a Nun.

**Strong's H5125 -** נוּן nûwn, noon; a primitive root; to resprout, i.e. propagate by shoots; figuratively, to be perpetual:—be continued., increase.

Abraham and his seed have indeed continued when so many other ancient peoples and kingdoms have disappeared. What God has promised, He will do, again and again.

**Luke 21:33** (TLV) Heaven and earth will pass away, but My words will never pass away.

**Genesis 17:8** (TLV) I will give to you and to your seed after you the land where you are an outsider—the whole land of Canaan—as an everlasting possession, and I will be their God.

**Genesis 24:7** (TLV) *Adonai*, the God of heaven, who took me from my father's house and from my native land and who spoke to me and made a pledge to me saying, 'To your seed I will give this land'—He will send His angel before you and you will take a wife for my son from there.

**God's Promise to Isaac** when he went to Gerar:

**Genesis 26:3-4** (TLV) Live as an outsider in this land and I will be with you and bless you—for to you and to your seed I give all these lands—and I will confirm my pledge that I swore to Abraham your father. 4 I will multiply your seed like the stars of the sky and I will give your seed all these lands. And in your seed all the nations of the earth will continually be blessed,

**God's Promise to Jacob** when he fled from his brother on the way to the house of wicked Laban:

**Genesis 28:1-4** (TLV) So Isaac called for Jacob, blessed him, commanded him and said to him, "Don't take a wife from the daughters of Canaan. 2 Get up, go to Paddan-aram, to the house of Bethuel, your mother's father, and take for yourself a wife from there, from the daughters of Laban, your mother's brother. 3 Now may *El Shaddai* bless you, and make you fruitful and multiply you so that you will become an assembly of peoples. 4 And may he give you the blessing of Abraham, to you and to your seed with you that you may take possession of the land of your sojourn, which God gave to Abraham."

**God reconfirmed that promise** again with an amazing vision of a ladder that reached into the heavens.

**Genesis 28:10-15** (TLV) Then Jacob left Beer-sheba and went toward Haran. 11 He happened upon a certain place and spent the night there, for the sun had set. So he took one of the stones from the place and put it by his head and lay down in that place. 12 He dreamed: All of a sudden, there was a stairway set up on the earth and its top reaching to the heavens—and behold, angels of God going up and down on it! 13 Surprisingly, *Adonai* was standing on top of it and He said, "I am *Adonai*, the God of your father Abraham and the God of Isaac. The land on which you lie, I will give it to you and to your seed. 14 Your seed will be as the dust of the land, and you will burst forth to the west and to the east and to the north and to the south. And in you all the families of the earth will be blessed—and in your seed. 15 Behold, I am with you, and I will watch over you wherever you go, and I will bring you back to this land, for I will not forsake you until I have done what I promised you."

After 20 years in the house of Laban, **God tells Jacob to leave and reconfirms the promise** of the Land as a gift of grace.

**Genesis 35:9-15** (TLV) God appeared to Jacob again, after he returned from Paddan-aram, and He blessed him. 10 God said to him: "Your name was Jacob. No longer will your name be Jacob, for your name will be Israel." So He named him Israel. 11 God also said to him: "I am *El Shaddai*. Be fruitful and multiply. A nation and an assembly of nations will come from you. From your loins will come forth kings. 12 The land that I gave to Abraham and to Isaac, I give it to you, and to your seed after you, I will give the land." 13 Then God went up from him at the place where He had spoken with him. 14 Jacob set up a memorial stone in the place where He had spoken with him—a stone pillar—and he poured a drink offering on it and poured oil on it. 15 Jacob named the place where God spoke with him

Beth-El.

So, now that we have seen the first mentions of the Promised Land connected to all the patriarchs, Abraham, Isaac, and Jacob, let's look at the first mention of Abram and see if we can discover his identity and who he is in relationship to the Jewish people of today.

In Genesis chapter 11 we are first introduced to Abram and his family as being in the genealogy of Eber, who is from the line of Noah's son Shem (Genesis 11:10).

**Genesis 11:16-17** (TLV) Eber lived 34 years and he fathered Peleg. 17 Eber lived 430 years after he fathered Peleg, and he fathered sons and daughters.

The genealogy listed in Genesis 11 goes like this:

1. Eber

2. Peleg

3. Reu

4. Serug

5. Nahor

6. Terah

**7. Abram** along with Nahor and Haran his brothers.

**Genesis 11:26-27** (TLV) Terah lived **70 years** when he fathered Abram, Nahor and Haran. 27 These are Terah's genealogies: Terah fathered Abram, Nahor and Haran. Haran fathered Lot.

Abram is listed as the 7th in the genealogy and was born when His father was 70. This maybe a coincidence, except we don't believe in coincidences when it comes to Scripture. Every number in the Bible has significance especially when we study and know what these numbers hint to. In this, case we can see that Abram being a "7th generation" is pointing to some type of "completion" or "rest" when Abram comes on the scene. The number 70 can be seen as a number relating to the nations. Abram will be called by God to be the "Father of Nations" and also the one from whom God will "make a great nation."

So, who is Eber? What does his name mean? The Strong's reference says: Eber or Heber = "the region beyond." This word is defined as the region from beyond usually situated across a stream or sea.

The root word for **Abram** is:

**H5676 עֵבֶר** 'êber, ay'-ber; from H5674; properly, a region across; but used only adverbially (with or without a preposition) on the opposite side (especially of the Jordan; usually meaning the east):— against, beyond, by, from, over, passage, quarter, (other, this) side, straight.

At first glance you might not think this is so significant, but as we begin to connect some dots or threads in Scripture, you will see how significant this "name" really is.

Now let's look at what Abram is called in Scripture. Remember, names in the Bible give us clues to identity and purpose.

**Genesis 14:13-16** (TLV) Then a survivor came and told Abram the Hebrew, who was dwelling by the large trees belonging to Mamre the Amorite, the brother of Eschol and the brother of Aner—they were Abram's allies. 14 When Abram heard that his kinsman had been taken captive, he rallied his trained men, those born in his household, 318 of them, and went in pursuit as far as Dan. 15 Then he divided his servants against them at night, and he defeated them and pursued them as far as Hovah, which is north of Damascus. 16 He brought back all the possessions, and also brought back his kinsman Lot and his possessions, as well as the women and the other people.

Abram is called a "Hebrew" by someone who had escaped in the war of the kings. Remember what we learned about Eber. His name means "one who came from beyond who crossed over a river or a stream."

Now look at the definition of a **Hebrew**, for it actually comes from the word "**Eber**."

**Strong's H5680** עִבְרִי 'Ibrîy, ib-ree'; patronymic from H5677; an Eberite (i.e. Hebrew) or descendant of Eber:—Hebrew(-ess, woman).

**Brown-Driver-Briggs Lexicon says:**
עִבְרִי adjective and name of a people **Hebrew**,
either **a**. put into the mouth of foreigners (Egyptian and Philistine), or **b**. used to distinguish Israel from foreigners (= *one from beyond, from the other side*, i.e. probably (in Hebrew tradition) *from beyond the Euphrates* (compare Joshua 24:2, 3), but possibly in fact (if name given in Cannan) *from beyond the Jordan*;

Abram the Hebrew was called that both because he was a descendant of Eber, but also because of his physical and spiritual journey to cross over the river Euphrates into the Land that God told him he would inherit. The rabbis look at

Abram's physical crossing over as pointing to the greater spiritual crossing over, out of idolatry and the ways of the nations, and into the worship of the true God who created the heavens and the earth. The Strong's definition hints that a "Hebrew" was the name that the nations, or Canaanites, would use to describe "one who came from beyond." Abraham the Hebrew was from the land of Mesopotamia. He lived in proximity to Babylon and Nimrod. In His day, Abram, at seventy-five years old, had an encounter with God and believed and trusted the God who appeared to him so deeply. He left everything familiar to embark on a journey of faith that is the foundation for all Believers today.

**Genesis 12:1-5** (TLV) Then *Adonai* said to Abram, "Get going out from your land, and from your relatives, and from your father's house, to the land that I will show you. 2 My heart's desire is to make you into a great nation, to bless you, to make your name great so that you may be a blessing. 3 My desire is to bless those who bless you, but whoever curses you I will curse, and in you all the families of the earth will be blessed. 4 So Abram went, just as *Adonai* had spoken to him. Also Lot went with him. (Now Abram was 75 years old when he departed from Haran.) 5 Abram took Sarai his wife, and Lot his nephew, and all their possessions that they had acquired, and the people that they acquired in Haran, and they left to go to the land of Canaan, and they entered the land of Canaan.

Abram is the first one to be called a Hebrew in the Bible, but that name will be used after this to describe the family of Abram over and over again. Even in the New Testament we have this amazing book called "Hebrews." The name has great spiritual connotation when you think every Believer in Yeshua has "crossed over" a spiritual barrier and divide to worship the God of Abraham, Isaac and Jacob. Every Believer in Him is a Spiritual Hebrew. Abraham, the first

Hebrew was told by God to "get going." The encounter with God was a "never turning back" moment for Abraham who understood somehow that God the Creator was going to do what He had promised no matter how impossible it looked.

Later, when Moses goes to Pharaoh and asks him to let God's people go and worship, look what he says:
**Exodus 9:1** (TLV) Then Adonai said to Moses, "Go in to Pharaoh, and tell him: This is what *Adonai*, the God of the Hebrews, says: 'Let My people go, so they may serve Me.'

The statement "Adonai (the Lord), God of the Hebrews" occurs 7 times in the Bible. It was the Hebrews that God came to deliver out of Egypt, and when anyone today gets delivered from spiritual Egypt, the realm of sin and death, they are reconnecting to the Hebrew people who were redeemed by the blood of the lamb thousands of years ago.

I encourage you at this point in the book, not to discount the relationship and connection you have to Abraham and his physical and spiritual descendants. As we get closer to the time when Messiah will return, the lines that have separated these descendants will be invisible and non-existent. I promise much more on this subject later, but we still have some more mining to do. We still haven't looked at the terms "Jew" or "Jewish."

**Romans 10:11-12** (TLV) For the Scripture says, "Whoever trusts in Him will not be put to shame." 12 For there is no distinction between Jew and Greek, for the same Lord is Lord of all—richly generous to all who call on Him. 13 For "Everyone who calls upon the name of *Adonai* shall be saved."

## Chapter One
### Group or Personal Study

1. Based on the scriptural evidence given in the Bible, do you agree that God gave to Abraham and his descendants what would eventually be called the Land of Israel? Please discuss or give references from this book or other Scriptures you have found concerning the Land of Israel.

_____
_____
_____
_____
_____

2. What have you learned or read about Abraham that inspires or challenges your personal faith?

_____
_____
_____
_____
_____

3. What do you think it would have been like to be like Abraham and leave your home and cleave to a God not made with hands?

_____
_____
_____
_____
_____

4. What have been some of the challenges you have had in sharing your faith in God with family or friends?

_____
_____
_____
_____
_____

5. Do you see from the Scriptures a connection to the Land as being a "gift of grace?"

_____
_____
_____
_____
_____

6. Why do you think God chose the Land of Canaan to give to Abraham and his descendants? Is there something inherently special about that Land versus other locations around the world?

_____
_____
_____
_____
_____

7. What does it mean to be a Hebrew? Can you find the Scripture in the New Testament about Paul proclaiming he is a Hebrew of Hebrews? Why would Paul still use the term Hebrew to describe himself?

_____
_____
_____
_____
_____

8. As a Believer in Messiah can you see yourself as a spiritual Hebrew? Why or why not?

_____

_____

_____

_____

_____

9. Are you beginning to see the Bible as more seamless, connecting the Old and the New Testaments as one story and one plan?

_____

_____

_____

_____

_____

10. What is the one thing that stands out to you from this first chapter that you can take and start applying to your life right now? What are some other "take-aways" that you need to dig in to and study more about?

# Chapter Two
## The Million Dollar Question –
## Who are These "Jews" and What Makes Them So Special?

If you go on the internet and do a search you will most likely not find what I am about to share with you. The question on who the Jewish people are is loaded with controversy, and can and has ignited arguments, fights and yes, even wars! Many today want to discount the term "Jew," being "Jewish," and the Jewish religion of "Judaism."

Many years ago, I began researching from the Scriptures to find, as you know, the first mention of "Jew," its proper context, and how the term continues to play out throughout the Bible. I could not even believe what I found, and I hope you see from the first mention, the tie in to the Land promised to Abraham and how these Jews have struggled from even before being called "Jews" with possessing, living in and having the good life that God promised them in this Land. I don't want to get ahead of myself, but when you see the Hebrew patriarchs Abraham, Isaac, and Jacob in their journeys and struggles, you have to realize that what they did as individuals is a preview and prophecy of their descendants later. This is how the rabbis view the Bible. That is another reason it's important to look at the first mention of everything in the Bible.

The patriarchs, with the exception of Isaac, were exiled from the Land and then came back to the Land. Isaac, the promised heir and beloved son of Abraham, was told by God not to go down and descend into Egypt, but stay in the Land and sow, even in the time of famine. Isaac became very blessed and reaped 100-fold while everyone else was in lack.

When you come to Messiah, He has promised to bless you and turn you away from all iniquity and sin. We are descendants of Abraham through Yeshua, and so we become heirs like Isaac and have an inheritance that will never be lost. Included in that inheritance is the Promised Land that was first given to Abraham. By faith, right now agree with me that what God has promised, He will do! He cannot lie! He is faithful to perform His Word and Covenant to one thousand generations.

**Psalms 105:8** (TLV) He remembers His covenant forever— the word He commanded for a thousand generations—

The first mention of the Hebrew word for "Jew" seems to occur in the Bible after the Southern Kingdom is taken captive and exiled from their land about 583 BC. It is here that we find the term "Jew" over and over again. We also see in the book of Esther that Mordecai was identified as a Jew who sat in the king's gate. He had been exiled in the Babylonian captivity. He is identified as "from the tribe of Benjamin and the province of Judah."

In the book of Esther, Haman calls Mordecai simply a "Jew." I have heard rabbis teach from the book of Esther, saying that being Jewish meant you were or had been a resident of the country of Judah, and that it really didn't matter if you were by bloodline or of a different Tribe than Judah.

According to Rabbi David Fohrman, if you lived or resided like Mordecai or Esther, his cousin, then you were a Jew. Now of course this is just one orthodox rabbi's opinion, but maybe he is on to something. A Jew can identify himself as being from or living in the land of Judah, and according to the Strong's Concordance, the term "Jew" after the Babylonian captivity can apply to any Tribe of Israel. By the way, the book of Esther is not the first mention of this term.

The Hebrew word for Jew actually seems to occur much earlier in the Scriptures. I do however, want you to see how the word "Jew" seems to always have some type of persecution or negativity tied to it.

**Esther 3:1-9** (TLV)  Some time later King Ahasuerus promoted Haman, son of Hammedatha the Agagite, elevating him and setting his chair above all the officials who were with him. 2 All the king's servants who were at the king's gate bowed down and paid honor to Haman, for the king had commanded it. But Mordecai would not bow down or pay him honor. 3 Then the king's servants who were at the king's gate said to Mordecai, "Why are you disobeying the king's command?" 4 Day after day, they spoke to him but he would not listen to them. Therefore they told Haman in order to see whether Mordecai's resolve would prevail, for he had told them that he was a Jew. 5 When Haman saw that Mordecai was not bowing down or paying him honor, Haman was filled with rage. 6 But it was repugnant in his eyes to lay hands on Mordecai alone, for they had told him the identity of Mordecai's people. So Haman sought to destroy all the Jews, the people of Mordecai, who were throughout the whole kingdom of Ahasuerus. 7 In the first month (that is the month of Nisan), in the twelfth year of King Ahasuerus, they cast the pur (that is, 'the lot') in the presence of Haman from day to day and month to month, up to the twelfth month, which is the month of Adar.
8 Haman then said to King Ahasuerus: "There is a certain people scattered and dispersed among the peoples in all the provinces of your kingdom whose laws differ from those of every other people and who do not obey the king's laws. It is not in the king's interest to tolerate them. 9 If it pleases the king, let an edict be written to destroy them. I will pay

10,000 talents of silver into the hands of those who carry out this business, to put it into the king's treasuries."

Can you see how Haman told the King about these "Jews" who did not really fit in or assimilate with the Persian empire's laws? He told the king that these "certain people" were not following the king's laws, but have their own laws. He basically said, "These Jews are everywhere and they are going to cause you trouble, so just get rid of them. I will even pay you to allow me to do it for you."

Now wicked Haman kind of said some half-truths. The Jews **were** dispersed, they **were** different, and they **do** follow Torah, which is God's instructions on how to live. What he **did not** tell the king is that these "certain people" were probably the most valuable citizens in the kingdom of Persia because they have to follow and obey God, which means they actually have to love their neighbors and honor those in authority.

Before we move on, let's look at the Hebrew word for **Jew** from the Strong's:

**H3064** יְהוּדִי Yᵉhûwdîy, yeh-hoo-dee'; patronymically from H3063; a Jehudite (i.e. Judaite or Jew), or descendant of Jehudah (i.e. Judah):—Jew.

**H3063** יְהוּדָה Yᵉhûwdâh, yeh-hoo-daw'; from H3034; celebrated; Jehudah (or Judah), the name of five Israelites; also of the tribe descended from the first, and of its territory:—Judah.

## Gesenius' Hebrew-Chaldee Lexicon

The root word is:

יְהוּדִי, pl. יְהוּדִים, sometimes יְהוּדִיִּים Est. 4:7; 8:1,
7, 13; 9:15, 18, in כתיב—

(1) Gent. noun, *a Jew*—(*a*) one who belonged to
the kingdom of Judah, 2 Ki. 16:6; 25:25.—(*b*) in
the later Hebrew, after the carrying away of the
ten tribes, it was applied to any Israelite, Jer. 32:12;
38:19; 40:11; 43:9; especially 34:9 (Syn. עִבְרִי).
Neh. 1:2; 3:33; 4:6; Est. 2:5; 3:4; 5:13. Fem.
יְהוּדִיָּה 1 Ch. 4:18.

(2) [*Jehudi*], pr. n. m. Jer. 36:14, 21.

**H3034** יָדָה **yâdâh,** yaw-daw'; a primitive root; used only as
denominative from H3027; literally, to use (i.e. hold out) the
hand; physically, to throw (a stone, an arrow) at or away;
especially to revere or worship (with extended hands);
intensively, to bemoan (by wringing the hands):—cast (out),
(make) confess(-ion), praise, shoot, (give) thank(-ful, -s,
-sgiving).

The KJV translates Strong's H3034 in the following manner:
praise (53x), give thanks (32x), confess (16x), thank (5x),
make confession (2x), thanksgiving (2x), cast (1x), cast
out (1x), shoot (1x), thankful (1x).

The Hebrew word for "Jew" is going to point us to a people
related to the kingdom of Judah. That is a good starting
place for us, but it's just the tip of the iceberg. The Hebrew
definitions are telling us that they are the people who at one
time made their home in the land of Judah, but who were
descendants from the actual Tribe of Judah?
We also learned from the Gesenius' Hebrew-Chaldee
Lexicon that after the exile of the Southern Kingdom of
Judah, any Israelite can be called a Jew, even if they had no
affiliation with the Land or the Tribe of Judah.

Can you see how confusing the term "Jew "can be? I want you to know that the definition of Jew has expanded even beyond that today, especially in the Land of Israel and in the Jewish religious and secular communities. Let's now try to find the first mention of the word "Jew" in the Bible and see if we can find some clues to why there might be some type of root in the blatant hatred many people have over the Jews.

The first mention of **H3064**:

**2 Kings 16:5-6** (TLV) Then King Rezin of Aram and Pekah son of King Remaliah of Israel marched against Jerusalem to wage war. They besieged Ahaz, but could not overcome him. 6 At that time King Rezin of Aram recovered Elath for Aram, and drove the **Jews** (H3064) out of Elath. Then the Edomites came to Elath and settled there to this day.

I don't know if you caught it, but King Elam was from Aram which is Syria. He drove out the Jews who had been living in Elath, and expelled them from that land. Then the Edomites came to Elath and made it their forever home! The first mention of "Jew" in Scripture has to do with a **land dispute**!

The Jews were made to leave the land they had been living in and they got replaced by the Edomites. During his reign, King Solomon had captured this place and put his fleet of ships there. He restored this territory to Judah, but this was disputed by King Elam of Syria who fought and got it back in his day (2 Kings 14:22).

Here is the crazy thing: this territory is returned again back to Judah during the reign of another king named Uzziah.

**2 Chronicles 26:1-2** (TLV) Then all the people of Judah took Uzziah, who was 16 years old, and made him king in place of his father Amaziah. 2 He built Eloth and restored it to Judah after the king slept with his fathers.

Can you see how the term "Jew" has its roots in a "**land dispute**" as its first mention in Scripture? I promise you I'm not making this up.

The first mention of Jews was when a Syrian king decided to give back Edom his land. Could this also point prophetically to what might be happening, or continues to happen, to the Land of Israel? Other nations come to fight against the Land of Israel to give some of it to those they think are the rightful owners, just like Syria did for the Edomites, the descendants of Esau.

Can you also see how anytime the term "Jew" is mentioned by those who don't love them or believe they have any rights to the Land, portray them as the evil occupiers; the people who stole the land from the "true natives" of the Land?

This rhetoric of demeaning anything related to the word "Jew" or being "Jewish" that we all continue to hear has its roots in the Bible text itself. We see this in the very first mention of "Jew" in the Bible. If you continue following the "Jew" throughout Scripture, even in the New Testament, you will find this same "bias" by those who either penned or have slanted the many translations of the Bible, and thus continuing to make the word "Jew" a very negative term, not just to the world at large, but to Christians who believe the Bible.

This negative connotation is the opposite of the true meaning of the root word for "Jew" which is "praise, to give thanks or to confess." Today people aren't thankful for the

Jews, and even some Christians say the Jews are guilty of killing their Messiah. How far have we gone from the Bible definition? How many times do you have to hear a false narrative to believe there is some truth behind it? This is the way the enemy works to get the world to "hate" anyone called a Jew, Jewish, and practices Judaism.

So how do we combat this negativity, slant and bias against the Jew? Perhaps the answer begins with a changed heart and mind that can come to anyone who will begin to be transformed as they renew their minds through God's Word. Perhaps equally as important is the power of prayer.

**Romans 12:1-2** (TLV) I urge you therefore, brothers and sisters, by the mercies of God, to present your bodies as a living sacrifice—holy, acceptable to God—which is your spiritual service. 2 Do not be conformed to this world but be transformed by the renewing of your mind, so that you may discern what is the will of God—what is good and acceptable and perfect.

So now let's dig a little deeper into what it means to be "Jewish." We learned the first mention of "Jew," but we have to go before that to see where that actually came from? If you are familiar with the Bible and the Old Testament you know that Abraham, Isaac, and Jacob were all Hebrews. Also, the third patriarch, Jacob would have 12 sons as well as have his name changed by God from Jacob to Israel after he left with all his family from his father-in-law Laban. So, at this point in history, this is where we can trace the foundation and beginning for the term "Jew." It is actually found in Jacob's fourth son named "Judah" through Leah.

**Genesis 29:35** (TLV) Then she became pregnant again and gave birth to a son and said, "This time I **praise (H3034)**

Adonai." For this reason she named him **Judah (H3063)**. Then she stopped having children.

**Praise H3034** is also the root word for **Judah H3063**.

According to the Brown- Driver- Briggs Lexicon:
Strong's H3034 **Hiph. *give thanks, confess* (originally *acknowledge?*)** is commonly derived, perhaps from gestures accompanying the act, see Thes LagOr. ii. 22, yet

connection uncertain; Aramaic Pa. יְדִי, Aph. אוֹדִי *Confess*

When Leah named her son Judah, she did so to praise God and be thankful to the Lord who gave her this fourth son. Every time she or someone would call out the name Judah, they would be making a confession and acknowledgement to be thankful or to praise God through that name. The name Judah seems to be a prophetic proclamation that one day all will confess and acknowledge and give thankful praise to God.

Another way of looking at **Genesis 29:35** could be:

"Then she became pregnant again and gave birth to a son and said, 'Now I am **thankful** to **confess** and **acknowledge** the Lord.' Therefore, she called his name Judah (and she **confessed** & **acknowledged** with **thankfulness** to the Lord)."

Remember we learned that, after the Babylonian captivity the individual Tribes were called "Jews." So, at the root level, every time we say "Jew," we are making a confession to acknowledge and thank and praise God at some level. Now look at the Hebrew letters that make up the name Judah.

י Yud

ה Hey

ו Vav

ד Dalet

ה Hey

יְהֹוָה In the four-letter name of God, we see all of these letters except one.

**H3068 יְהֹוָה Y<sup>e</sup>hôvâh,** yeh-ho-vaw'; from H1961; (the) self-Existent or Eternal; Jeho-vah, Jewish national name of God:—Jehovah, the Lord. Compare H3050, H3069.

י Yud

ה Hey

ו Vav

ה Hey

What is the missing letter in God's name given to Judah? It is the Dalet.

ד Dalet has a numerical value of 4 and is the symbol for "door." Now how amazing is this? The only letter not in YHVH- Adonai's name, is the Dalet. The only way to confess and acknowledge the Lord and His Messiah will be through the "door" of Tribe of Judah (the Jew or Jewish people.)

**John 10:1-9** (TLV) "Amen, amen I tell you, he who does not enter the sheepfold by the door, but climbs in some other way, is a thief and a robber. 2 But he who enters through the door is the shepherd of the sheep. 3 To him the doorkeeper opens, and the sheep hear his voice. The shepherd calls his own sheep by name and leads them out. 4 "When he has brought out all his own, he goes ahead of them; and the sheep follow him because they know his voice. 5 They will never follow a stranger, but will run away from him, for they do not know the voice of strangers." 6 Yeshua told them this parable, but they did not understand what He was telling them. 7 So Yeshua said again, "Amen, amen I tell you, I am the gate for the sheep. 8 All those who came before Me are thieves and robbers, but the sheep did not listen to them. 9 I am the door! If anyone comes in through Me, he will be saved. He will come and go and find pasture.

Judah is 4th in birth order which also points to the 4th letter of the Hebrew alphabet, the Dalet or Door. But there's more to this because Judah is not in any way the first born of Jacob/Israel, yet Scripture, prophecy and the blessings spoken over this 4th son of Jacob confirms his seed to be the line of the Messiah and King.

**Genesis 49:8** Judah, so you are—your brothers will praise you: Your hand will be on your enemies' neck. Your father's sons will bow down to you.

In Genesis chapter 49 we find Jacob/Israel's prophetic blessings over his children. The most amazing thing is it hints to the destinies of these sons of Jacob whom later will be called the Tribes of Israel. Now notice how, even though Judah is not the first born, and he has no greater birthright in the natural, he is told by Jacob that his father's children will bow before him. This is a preview of how a King will come from Judah, and not just any king, but One that will rule over, not only all the Tribes, but all the world.

Look at the first part of the blessing. It describes Judah as the one whom his brothers shall "confess or acknowledge." This is why today all descendants of Jacob-Israel call themselves Jews. They are "acknowledging and confessing" this prophecy of Jacob. They do this willingly, and sometimes might I add, with a pride of being called "of Jewish descent." Thus, we can see that from the blessing on Judah, the rest of the Tribes will "confess" and "acknowledge" their identity through the Tribe of Judah.

Let's look and see how the blessing is continued throughout the Scriptures.

**Genesis 49:8-10** (AMP) "Judah, you are the one whom your brothers shall praise; Your hand will be on the neck of your enemies; Your father's sons shall bow down to you. 9 "Judah, a lion's cub; With the prey, my son, you have gone high up [the mountain]. He stooped down, he crouched like a lion, And like a lion—who dares rouse him? 10 "The scepter [of royalty] shall not depart from Judah, Nor the ruler's staff from between his feet, Until Shiloh [the Messiah, the Peaceful One] comes, And to Him shall be the obedience of the peoples.

Judah is mentioned as the cub of a lion and even a lioness. Is there any doubt what animal is "king of the jungle?" The Amplified version of this Scripture lets us know very clearly that the blessing spoken by Jacob upon Judah is a blessing of rulership. A prophecy of Messiah is in this very passage and is acknowledged by the Jewish Sages as well.

Did you know that rulership is also tied to the number 4? In the fourth day of Creation, God creates the sun and the moon to rule over the day and the night. The Hebrew word for "rule" is also sometimes translated as "to govern." Judah will be the Tribe to establish God's government in the earth. When Messiah comes, the people will bow and be obedient to His rule and authority. Maybe being the 4th in birth order was not an accident, but a prophecy of God's government coming to the earth through the Tribe of Judah.

The Scripture in Genesis 49:10 using the word Shiloh is one of great disputes. Here are some of what I found among Jewish writings and understanding of this:

[1] עד כי יבא שילה means until the King Messiah will come, whose will be the kingdom (Genesis Rabbah 99:8). Thus too does Onkelos render it. A Midrashic interpretation is: שילה is the same as שי לו, a present unto him, as it is said, (Psalms 76:12) "Let them bring (שי) presents unto him that is to be feared."

[2] ולו יקהת עמים means AND UNTO HIM [SHALL BE] AN ASSEMBLAGE OF PEOPLES.too, a root יָקַה to assemble, as שמחה the construct of which is שמחת from שמח) — an assembly of nations. And so it is actually said with reference to the Messiah, (Isaiah 11:10) "Unto him shall the nations seek".

[3]A sampling of other explanations:

---------------

[1]https://www.sefaria.org/Genesis.49.10? lang=bi&with=Rashi&lang2=en

[2]https://www.sefaria.org/Genesis.49.10? lang=bi&with=Rashi&lang2=en

[3] https://judaism.stackexchange.com/questions/4548/whats-the-meaning-of-shiloh-in-the-last-blessing-of-yaakov-on-his-children

- It comes from the word שלו - the one to whom kingship belongs. Or, alternately, from שי לו - the one to whom presents will be brought. (Rashi)
- It's from שלה, "to give birth," or שליה, "amniotic sac." So it means "the son, or descendant, of Yehudah." (Ramban; Ibn Ezra; Rabbeinu Bechayei - who also adds, possibly with a view to countering non-Jewish distortions of this verse, that the Torah is stressing that Moshiach is a regular human being, born of a woman exactly like everyone else.)
- The two words יבא שילה have the same numerical value as משיח. (Baal Haturim)
- It's from שלום, "peace," and also שולים, "hems" (the ends or lowest parts of a garment), so it means "the final and lasting peace" of history (Sforno).

- Variation on this: it's from שולים only, and means "[Moshiach will come, unexpectedly,] when the Jewish People are at their lowest ebb" (R' S.R. Hirsch).

Because we are studying prophecy, we always seek to go back to Holy Scripture as the foundation for everything. Let's look at the word in question in its context.

Gesenius' Hebrew-Chaldee Lexicon

**H7886 שִׁילֹה Shîylôh,** shee-lo'; from H7951; tranquil; Shiloh, an epithet of the Messiah:—Shiloh.

The root word for Shiloh is about prosperity, security and happiness.

**H7951 שָׁלָה shâlâh,** shaw-law'; or שָׁלַו shâlav; (Job 3:26), a primitive root; to be tranquil, i.e. secure or successful:—be happy, prosper, be in safety.

שִׁילֹה —(1) *tranquillity, rest;* from the root שָׁלָה of the form פִּישׁוֹר, קִיטוֹר; and if a derivative of a verb לה be wanted, גָּלָה from the root גָּלָה. This power of the word seems to be that which it has in the much discussed passage, Gen. 49:10, "the sceptre shall not depart from Judah עַד כִּי־יָבֹא שִׁילֹה וְלֹו ... יִקְּהַת עַמִּים until tranquillity shall come, and the peoples shall obey him (Judah). Then let him bind," etc.; i. e. Judah shall not lay down the sceptre of the ruler, until his enemies be subdued, and he shall rule over many people; an expectation belonging to the kingdom of the Messiah, who was to spring from the tribe of Judah. Others whom I followed in edit. 1, take שִׁילֹה in this passage as a concrete, and render it *the peaceable one, peace-maker;* either understanding the Messiah (compare שַׂר שָׁלֹום Isa. 9:5), or Solomon (compare שְׁלֹמֹה 1 Ch. 22:9); so the Samaritans (see Repert. f. bibl. und morgenländ. Litt. xvi. 168). The ancient versions take שִׁלֹה (שֶׁלֹה) as being compounded of שֶׁ i. q. אֲשֶׁר and לֹה i. q. לֹו to him in this sense, " until he shall come to whom the sceptre, the dominion belongs," i. e. Messiah (comp. Eze. 21:32, עַד־בֹּא אֲשֶׁר־לֹו הַמִּשְׁפָּט LXX. ᾧ καθήκει). LXX. in several copies, τὰ ἀποκείμενα αὐτῷ, "the things which are reserved for him" (others with Symm.); ᾧ ἀπόκειται, he "for whom it is reserved." Syr. Saad., "he whose it is." Targ. Onk. "Messiah, whose is the kingdom." There is also a variety in the reading (שִׁלֹה in several codd. and editt.; שָׁלֹה in twenty-eight Jewish manuscripts, and in all the Samaritan, שִׁלֹו in a few codd.); but this three-fold manner is of but little moment in this passage, as the same variety is found in the pr. n. (No. 2). This only follows from it, that the Hebrew critics and copyists writing שִׁילֹה took it for a simple word, and not as the old interpreters, as a compound. [The older copies, however, do read שָׁלֹה.] The opinions of theologians on this passage have been collected by Hengstenberg, Christologie d. A. T. i. p. 59, seqq.

(2) ("place of rest"), [*Shiloh*], pr. n. of a town of the Ephraimites, situated on a mountain to the north of Bethel, where the holy tabernacle was set for some time, Josh. 18:1; 1 Sam. 4:3. It is variously written שִׁילֹו Jud. 21:21; Jer. 7:12; שִׁלֹו Jud. 21:19; 1 Sa. 1:24; 3:21; שִׁלֹה Josh. 18:1, 8; 1 Sa. 1:3, 9; 1 Ki. 2:27. [Now prob. Seilûn سیلون Rob. iii. 85.]

**Psalm 122:6** (WEB) Pray for the peace of Jerusalem. Those who love you will **prosper. (H7951)**

Jerusalem is the City of Peace, but we are told to pray for it and love it so we will be secure and prosperous.

Here are some final comments concerning Shiloh I found.

[4]*The school of Rebbe Shilo says 'Shilo' is his name as it says "Until Shilo Comes." (Genesis 49:10) Rashi has no comment here, but we see that the Midrash sees 'Shilo' as the name of a person. Here is the full verse: The scepter shall not depart from Judah, nor the student of the law from between his feet, until Shiloh comes, and to him will be a gathering of peoples.*

On the words used in the Talmud Rashi says the following: **until Shiloh comes**: *[This refers to] the King Messiah, to whom the kingdom belongs (שֶׁלוֹ) , and so did Onkelos render it: [until the Messiah comes, to whom the kingdom belongs]. According to the Midrash Aggadah, ["Shiloh" is a combination of] שַׁי לוֹ, a gift to him, as it is said:"they will bring a gift to him who is to be feared" (Ps. 76:12). - [From Gen. Rabbah ed. Theodore-Albeck p. 1210 ] Notice that the passage in the Talmud is not the source for saying it refers to the Messiah. His primary source is Onkelos, whose translations/comments are always trying to reflect the parashat. Onkelos reaches this conclusion because if we look at the whole passage in its context, i.e. the blessings Yakov gives to his children, we see that they are referring to* **end-times/Messianic events,** *as it states explicitly in verse 1 of the chapter: Jacob called for his sons and said, "Gather and I will tell you what will happen to you at the* **end of days**.

---

[4] http://judaismsanswer.com/midrash2.htm

From both the Hebrew word and what we learn from ancient commenters like Rashi and the Aramaic translation by Onkelos, we can see they all agree that **Shiloh is a prophecy of Messiah,** who will receive gifts worthy of a king, but will also be the One that provides prosperity, peace and security to those who obey Him as the ultimate Law Giver.

You who are familiar with the New Testament can now connect the birth of Messiah who was heralded at His birth with "Peace on Earth and goodwill to men." Do you remember how Messiah was brought presents in a similar way to Rashi's understanding of the word Shiloh?

**Matthew 2:11** TLV And when they came into the house, they saw the Child with His mother Miriam; and they fell down and worshiped Him. Then, opening their treasures, they presented to Him gifts of gold, frankincense, and myrrh.

# Chapter Two

## Group or Personal Study

1. The first mention of the Jew in Scripture has to do with a"
_____.

2. What is the missing letter in God's name given to
"Judah"? It is the _____

3. Write down some of the meanings of the term "Judah" in
the Hebrew language?
_____
_____
_____
_____
_____

4. According to the rabbis, what did "being Jewish" mean
during the time of the book of Esther? Please explain.
_____
_____
_____
_____
_____

5. What number is the birth order of Judah?
_____
_____
_____
_____
_____

6 What is that number tied to or hinted to in the Scriptures
from the Creation story?

_____
_____
_____

_____

_____

7. According to Jacob's blessing and prophecy over his son Judah, what does the Bible say Judah's brothers will do?

_____

_____

_____

_____

_____

8. Describe the blessings of Genesis 49 over Judah. Do you see it as a Messianic Prophecy? If so, why?

_____

_____

_____

_____

_____

9. Does the word Shiloh according to Rashi have to do with Messiah? If so, what does he say the Hebrew word for Shiloh actually means?

_____

_____

_____

_____

_____

10. Can you connect Yeshua declaring Himself as the Door to the Hebrew word for Jew? What letter in the Hebrew has the symbol of a door?

_____

_____

_____

_____

# Chapter Three
## Why Should Every Believer Pray for,
## Seek to Bless and
## Love the Jewish People?

Now let's go back to why God called Abraham and ultimately his descendants, the Jews. Was God wanting a people that would rule and dominate the world? Did He call Abraham to curse or harm the world in any way? What did we learn about Abraham's calling from God? We learned that it would be through his seed that all the families on the earth would be blessed, because Abraham and the Jewish people are all called to be a blessing!

The Jew does have a special place and unique role, but it does not mean they are to be worshipped or for anyone to feel jealous because of God's sovereign call for them. The greater the calling, the greater the responsibility a person has to God to fulfill that mission. This is why perhaps the judgments over the history of the Jewish people seem to be harsh. Let's pray for them to fulfill and embrace that calling, to be the Light to the nations the way Abraham began when he left all to follow Adonai's call. Just like Abraham was asked to go on a journey by faith, each one of us has been connected to that calling. If you are reading this book, it is because somewhere deep down inside you want to know what your role is on how you should treat Jewish people. If you are not born Jewish or can't find a blood or physical connection, don't feel slighted. You too, have a very important role. We will be looking at that in the next chapter, and you can be sure it is not a small or insignificant calling.

So, what is so special about the Jews? Why should we be praying for them? Let's dig into this subject a little further. Believe me, I do realize how difficult this is for many people, especially Christian Believers who have been taught unknowingly some type of replacement teaching or theology. Most people not only have been taught this in some way and have no idea that they have been, what I like to call, "hacked." As you read this book, I want you to realize that God has a forever plan for Abraham and his descendants, the Jewish people. They never get swapped-out or replaced by a new breed of people. The people who have physically descended from Father Abraham have been given a divine mission and mandate in the world, and also a blessing that is to continue to flow and grow to every city, family, and nation. Some of this replacement teaching might be in a different form and sound something like, "*These Jews have already done the mission and plan God had because we already have the Messiah. Jesus came to bring the Good News of His death, burial, and resurrection. He said, 'It is finished,' so now God is finished with the Jews and the Law. It's all about the born-again people, not those unbelieving Jews.*"

Before we go on to another chapter, let's be very clear about what God said about the Jews and Israel.

**Deuteronomy 7:6-11** (TLV) For you are a holy people to Adonai your God—from all the peoples on the face of the earth, Adonai your God has chosen you to be His treasured people. 7 "It is not because you are more numerous than all the peoples that Adonai set His love on you and chose you—for you are the least of all peoples. 8 Rather, because of His love for you and His keeping the oath He swore to your fathers, Adonai brought you out with a mighty hand and redeemed you from the house of slavery, from the hand of Pharaoh king of Egypt. 9 "Know therefore that Adonai your God, He is God—the faithful God who keeps covenant kindness for a thousand generations with those who love Him and keep His mitzvot, 10 but repays those who hate Him to their face, to annihilate them. He will not hesitate with him who hates Him; He will repay him to his face. 11

Therefore you are to keep the commandment—both the statutes and the ordinances—that I am commanding you today, to do them.

Do you think God has somehow stopped loving these people? Did these same people become unchosen or no longer a treasure to God? Has the thousand generational covenant somehow run its course and is now finished? Is God no longer faithful and did His kindness somehow get spent all up and is no longer available to these people who were chosen by God's sovereign will?

Did you know 10 times in the Exodus story of the Bible, God said to Pharaoh, **"Let My people go?"** When God said that, did He really mean it? Were the people really God's chosen people and nation? If they were God's people during the Exodus, are they somehow not God's people anymore?

Let's look at some more Scriptures that will help solidify the "forever" covenant for the Jewish people. (All emphasis mine.)

**Leviticus 26:12** (TLV) I will walk among you and will be your God, and **you will be My people.**

**2 Chronicles 7:14** (WEB) **If my people**, who are called by my name, will humble themselves, pray, seek my face, and turn from their wicked ways, then I will hear from heaven, will forgive their sin, and will heal their land.

**Jeremiah 12:15-17** (TLV) Yet it will come to pass, after I have uprooted them, that I will again have compassion on them and I will bring them back, each one to his inheritance and each one to his land. 16 "So it will come to pass, if they will diligently learn the ways of **My people**—to swear by My Name, 'As *Adonai* lives,' just as they taught **My people** to swear by Baal—then they will be built up in the midst of **My people.** 17 But if they will not obey, then I will uproot that nation, plucking it up and destroying it." It is a declaration of *Adonai*.

When the nations cause Israel to go astray, they also will be judged, but if they learn the ways of God's people, they will be built up among them. This is a prophecy of the sheep and goat nations that Yeshua Himself talked about. The nations that align and bless Israel will not only be spared, but built. Those who refuse to align themselves will be plucked up and destroyed.

**Isaiah 51:1-16** (TLV) "Listen to Me, you who pursue justice, you who seek *Adonai*. Look to the rock from which you were hewn, and to the quarry from which you were dug. 2 **Look to Abraham your father and to Sarah who bore you.** For when I called him, he was but one, then I blessed him and multiplied him." 3 For *Adonai* will comfort Zion. He will comfort all her waste places. He will make her wilderness like Eden, her desert like the garden of *Adonai*. Joy and gladness will be found in her, thanksgiving and a sound of melody. 4 "Pay attention to Me, My people, give ear to Me, My nation. For *Torah* will go out from Me, My justice as a light to the peoples.5 My righteousness is near, My salvation has gone out, and My arms will judge the nations. The coastlands will wait for Me— for My arm they will wait expectantly. 6 Lift up your eyes to the heavens, and look at the earth beneath. For the heavens will vanish like smoke, the earth will wear out like a garment, and its inhabitants will die like gnats, but My salvation will be forever, and My righteousness never wane. 7 Listen to Me, you who know justice, a people with My *Torah* in their heart: Do not fear the taunt of men, nor be dismayed at their insults. 8 For the moth will eat them like a garment, and the worm will eat them like wool. But My righteousness will be forever and My salvation for all generations." 9 Awake, awake, put on strength, O arm of *Adonai*, awake, as in days of old, the generations of long ago. Was it not You who cut Rahab in pieces, who pierced the dragon? 10 Was it not You who dried up the sea, the waters of the great deep, who made the depths of the sea a path for the redeemed to pass over? **11 Now the ransomed of *Adonai* will return, and come to Zion with singing.** Everlasting joy will be upon their heads. They will obtain gladness and joy, and sorrow and sighing will flee away. 12 "I, I am the One who comforts you. Who are you that you should fear man, who dies, or a son of man, who is given up like grass?" 13 **But you forgot *Adonai* your Maker,** who stretched out the heavens and laid the foundations of the earth. Are you in constant dread all day because of the fury of the oppressor as he makes ready to destroy? But where is the fury of the oppressor? 14 Soon one bowed down will be released. He will not die and go to the Pit, nor will his bread be lacking. 15 "For I am *Adonai* your God, who stirs up the sea so that its waves roar — *Adonai-Tzva'ot* is His Name. 16 I have put My words in your mouth, and covered you with the shadow of My hand — I who set the heavens in place, who laid the foundations of the earth, and say to Zion, **'You are My people.'"**

**Ezekiel 14:11** (TLV) so that the house of Israel will not wander again from Me or defile themselves again with all their transgressions. They will be **My people** and I will be their God." It is a declaration of *Adonai*.

**Psalm 81:9-17** (TLV) **Hear, My people,** I will admonish you — if you would listen to Me, O Israel! 10 Let there be no foreign god among you, and you shall not worship any alien god. 11 I am *Adonai* your God, who brought you up out of the land of Egypt. Open your mouth wide and I will fill it. 12 But My people did not listen to My voice. Israel was not willing to be Mine. 13 So I gave them over to the stubbornness of their heart, to walk in their own counsels.

14 Oh that My people would listen to Me, that Israel would walk in My ways! 15 I would soon subdue their enemies, and turn My hand against their foes. 16 Those who hate *Adonai* would cringe before Him— their time of doom would be forever. 17 But you would be fed with the finest wheat, with honey out of a rock would I satisfy you."

**Psalm 94:14** (TLV) For Adonai will not forsake His people. He will never abandon His inheritance.

Now let's also look at the New Testament and see if we can find out if God has forsaken His people and has changed His mind about them.

**Romans 11:1-2a** (TLV) I say then, has God **cast away** His people? Certainly not! For I also am an Israelite, of the seed of Abraham, of the tribe of Benjamin. 2 God has not **cast away** His people whom He foreknew.

**CAST AWAY**: G683 ἀπωθέομαι **apōthéomai,** ap-o-theh'-om-ahee; from G575 and the middle voice of ὠθέω ōthéō or ὤθω óthō (to shove); to push off, figuratively, to reject:—cast away, put away (from), thrust away (from).

**Vines Expository Dictionary:**
Cast: "to thrust away" (apo, "away," otheo, "to thrust"), in the NT used in the Middle Voice, signifying "to thrust from oneself, to cast off, by way of rejection," Act 7:27, 39; 13:46; Rom 11:1, 2; 1Ti 1:19.

In the book of Acts, we find the protocol of Believers in that day. Who were they supposed to spread the Good News to first?

**Acts 1:8** (AMP) But you will receive power *and* ability when the Holy Spirit comes upon you; and you will be My witnesses [to tell people about Me] both in **Jerusalem** and in all Judea, and Samaria, and even to the ends of the earth."

**Romans 1:16** (TLV) For I am not ashamed of the Good News, for it is the power of God for salvation to everyone who trusts—**to the Jew first** and also to the Greek.

**Romans 2:9-10** (CJB) Yes, he will pay back misery and anguish to every human being who does evil, to the **Jew first**, then to the Gentile; 10 but glory and honor and *shalom* to everyone who keeps doing what is good, to the **Jew first**, then to the Gentile.


I find it very interesting that God chooses the most educated Jew to bring the Good News and teaching of the Way of Messiah to those coming from the nations. Apostle or Rabbi Paul did not back off from his heritage, but he called himself a Hebrew of Hebrews, and although he put no confidence in his flesh, God used his training to bring a revolution for the Kingdom of God that started in Jerusalem, but eventually would go to the ends of the earth. Not only does God not cast away HIs people, they are going to be fully restored to their priestly mission to the Nations in the book of Revelation chapter 14 (*144,0000 12 Tribes*). The gifts and callings are without repentance and no one can change God's mind about what He has already decided and purposed. The Jewish people and the Land of Israel is what every believer must remember to keep their spiritual and physical eyes on. They have not been forsaken or cast away, and it is important that those grafted in remember the blessing and people they are grafted to. If you haven't read my book "Hacked," I highly recommend you read it to understand the true Gospel and what grafting really means.

**Romans 3:1-4** (OJB) What then is the advantage of the Yehudi (**Jew**)? Or what is the value of the bris milah (**covenant of circumcision**)? 2 Much in every way! For, koidem kol (**in the first place**), they are entrusted with the Divrei Hashem (**the oracles, the words of God**).

Now look how the Amplified Version translates this verse:

**Romans 3:1-4** (AMPC) Then what **advantage** remains to the **Jew?** [How is he favored?] Or what is the value or benefit of circumcision? 2 **Much in every way**. To begin with, to the Jews were entrusted the oracles (the brief communications, the intentions, the utterances) of God.

The Apostle Paul says there is a great and abundant advantage in every way to being a Jew and the Covenant of Circumcision. If this is really true, and Paul meant what he said, why does the Bible seem to teach the opposite to what Paul is saying here. The Greek words used for "advantage" and "every way" have to do with abundance and exceeding amounts.

**Advantage G4053 περισσός perissós,** per-is-sos'; from G4012 (in the sense of beyond); superabundant (in quantity) or superior (in quality); by implication, excessive; adverbially (with G1537) violently; neuter (as noun) preeminence: — exceeding abundantly above, more abundantly, advantage, exceedingly, very highly, beyond measure, more, superfluous, vehement(-ly).

Thayer's Greek Lexicon states: "1 over and above, more than is necessary, superadded"

**"Much in every way…"**

**Every G4183 πολύς polýs**, pol-oos'; including the forms from the alternate πολλός pollós; (singular) much (in any respect) or (plural) many; neuter (singular) as adverbial, largely; neuter (plural) as adverb or noun often, mostly, largely: — abundant, + altogether, common, + far (passed, spent), (+ be of a) great (age, deal, -ly, while), long, many, much, oft(-en (-times)), plenteous, sore, straitly. Compare G4118, G4119.

I promise I am not making this up. I am only showing you the Greek language for what Paul says about the Jews. Being Jewish is, in Paul's mind, very positive and is a great advantage. I want to submit to you that being a Jew has advantages, but they are not for lording over or dominating, but rather to be an example and a blessing to those who did not have that natural or spiritual legacy. Paul is not telling anyone to worship the Jew, but he is letting his audience know that they will always have a special place in the Kingdom. Today, many Jewish people do not know the Messiah Yeshua because they are under a partial blindness until the "fulness of the nations" comes in to the family of Abraham. This should behoove us all to continue to pray that God would remove the blindness and stumbling blocks that have kept them from their Messiah.

**Matthew 9:37** Then saith he unto his disciples, The harvest truly *is* plenteous, **G4183** but the labourers *are* few;

The Apostle Paul understood, like all New Testament writers, that God was not only **not** done with the Jews, but Yeshua did **not** come to start a new religion or a new way of following the God who appeared to Abraham back in Genesis chapter 12. God took the most able Torah scholar to teach those who were coming from the nations, the Lost Tribes, and the natural-born Jews, all the same teachings that had been passed down from centuries. This is why you hear Paul stating multiple times to hold on to the traditions. These were "Jewish" traditions. These were taught and modeled, many from the time before Nehemiah and the exile of the Southern Kingdom. These traditions were taken for granted back in Yeshua's day, but today we think that is just "Jewish" stuff that we Christians don't need to do because Jesus fulfilled everything now, and we don't need to do any of these traditions or the Torah, etc. etc. etc.

Why was Paul so adamant about tradition? Why were his letters to be passed to all the congregations? If the great Apostle-Rabbi Paul was teaching this after the resurrection, what did he know that we have forgotten or not learned?

**Galatians 1:13-16** (TLV) For you have heard of my earlier behavior in Judaism—how I persecuted God's community beyond measure and tried to destroy it. 14 I was even advancing within Judaism beyond many my own age among my people, **being a more extreme observer of my fathers' traditions.** 15 But when God—who set me apart from birth and called me through His grace—was pleased 16 to reveal His Son to me so I would proclaim Him among the Gentiles,

The Apostle Paul knew very well and practiced the Jewish traditions. Somehow God thought this was the guy necessary to teach those who were coming from the nations into the Kingdom. We never find Paul saying he stopped doing them. It seems Paul understood that as long as a tradition confirms the Word and your relationship to God, and has been passed down from the spiritual fathers and mothers, then it is to be continued.

**Colossians 4:16** (TLV) When this letter has been read among you, make sure that it is also read in Messiah's community of Laodicea. In turn, you should read my letter coming from Laodicea.

**2 Thessalonians 2:14-15** (TLV) He called you to this salvation through our proclaiming the Good News, for you to gain the glory of our Lord *Yeshua* the Messiah. 15 So then, brothers and sisters, stand firm and hold on to the **traditions** which you were taught, whether by word of mouth or by our letter.

Paul, like Yeshua, understood there were traditions that help you stay on God's path, and other traditions that keep you from God's path.

**Traditions: G3862 παράδοσις parádosis**, par-ad'-os-is; from G3860; transmission, i.e. (concretely) a precept; specially, the Jewish traditionary law:—ordinance, tradition.

**2 Thessalonians 3:6** (TLV) Now we command you, brothers and sisters, in the name of our Lord *Yeshua* the Messiah, to keep away from every brother who behaves irresponsibly and not according to the **<u>tradition</u>** they received from us.

As far as Paul was concerned, these traditions were such a part of the congregation that those who refused them should be withdrawn from. I want to submit to you that many of the traditions that we in the past have considered to be strictly Jewish are much more than realized. Because of the constant bombardment against anything Jewish, we must renew our minds and change our vocabulary to look at these traditions, not as just Jewish, but Kingdom Culture.

Look at the Greek word that Paul used for "holding" the traditions. Obviously, he thinks holding these traditions is life and not death!

**G2902 HOLD κρατέω** kratéō, krat-eh'-o; from G2904; to use strength, i.e. seize or retain (literally or figuratively): — hold (by, fast), keep, lay hand (hold) on, obtain, retain, take (by).

In the book of Revelation, those who are holding tightly to the commandments and the Testimony of Yeshua are the ones that eventually overcome the enemy.

**Revelations 12:17** (TLV) So the dragon became enraged at the woman and went off to make war with the rest of her offspring—those who keep the commandments of God and hold to the testimony of *Yeshua*.

These traditions are part of the testimony of Yeshua. They are evidence that we hold to His commandments and believe He taught the Way of Messiah, for whosoever will believe it. As long as the tradition did not contradict or replace the Word of God, Yeshua did not oppose them.

**Mark 7:8** (TLV) Having left behind the commandment of God, you hold on to the tradition of men."

**Revelation 14:12** (AMP) Here is [encouragement for] the steadfast endurance of the saints (God's people), those who *habitually* keep God's commandments and their faith in Jesus.

The commandments of God must be guarded and held tightly by God's beloved children. The many Kingdom traditions passed down help us stay aligned to the Spirit and Truth of the Word. I know we gave a lot of information in this chapter, but I hope it becomes revelational and revolutionary in the way you think and live as you begin to embrace these truths.

## Chapter Three
### Group or Personal Study

1. What are some New Testament Scriptures that confirm to you that God is not finished with the Jewish people? Please write them down and discuss or meditate on them.

_____
_____
_____
_____
_____

2. What did God mean when He called Israel His people? Can you find any Scriptural evidence that they are still God's people? Please explain?

_____
_____
_____
_____
_____

3. What does it mean to you to be called God's people? Does that imply any greater responsibilities? What are some responsibilities that go with that high calling?

_____
_____
_____
_____
_____

4. Have you been taught that God is finished with Israel and the Jewish people? Were you taught that all the bad things like the Holocaust happened because of their rejection of Messiah?

_____
_____
_____

_____

_____

5. Based on the Scriptures, has God cast away and forsaken Israel and the Jewish people? List some scriptures that confirm your findings.

_____

_____

_____

_____

_____

6. Being a Jew according to Paul has great advantages. What are they?

_____

_____

_____

_____

_____

7. Does the Bible want the other nations to worship the Jewish people, or pray that they fulfill their divine mission to be a _____ to the other nations?

8. What are some reasons Paul was so adamant about keeping the traditions? Did he expect all Believers, even those not born Jewish to do them? What does the Word say about doing these traditions?

_____

_____

_____

_____

_____

9. Do you think Yeshua was against all traditions, or just when it was in opposition to the Word instead of confirming it?

_____
_____
_____
_____
_____

**Mark 7:4-13** (TLV) And when they come from the marketplace, they do not eat unless they perform a ritual washing. There are many other traditions they have received and hold, such as the washing of cups, pitchers, copper vessels.) 5 The Pharisees and Torah scholars questioned Yeshua, "Why don't Your disciples walk according to the tradition of the elders? Why do they eat bread with unwashed hands?" 6 And He said to them, "Rightly did Isaiah prophesy about you hypocrites, as it is written, 'This people honors Me with their lips but their heart is far from Me. 7 And in vain they worship Me, teaching as doctrines the commandments of men.8 ' Having left behind the commandment of God, you hold on to the tradition of men." 9 He was also telling them, "You set aside the commands of God, in order that you may validate your own tradition. 10 For Moses said, 'Honor your father and your mother,' and, 'He who speaks evil of father or mother must be put to death.' 11 But you say if anyone tells his father or mother, 'Whatever you might have gained from me is korban (that is, an offering to God),' 12 then you no longer permit him to do anything for his father or mother, 13 making void the word of God with your tradition that you've handed down. And you do many such things."

10. What is this Scripture saying in light of this chapter?

_____
_____
_____
_____
_____

# Chapter Four:
## The Fig Tree and The Watchmen

If you are not born Jewish or can't trace any of your physical or natural roots back to Father Abraham, this chapter is for you! You see as we learned before, Abraham's mission and calling was to be a blessing to the families and nations of the earth. Once these families and nations understand their calling and mission, they will no longer feel a separation between them and the Jewish people and the Land of Israel. It wasn't long ago I heard an amazing teaching from a Messianic rabbi about this subject. Rabbi Shapira shared how it was the Believers in Yeshua's job from the nations to now pray and bless the Jewish people and the Land of Israel, because it is what the Bible has commanded them to do. Since the recent war in Gaza on October 7, 2023, many Believers in the Lord have not been able to rightly discern their role and mission. I hope this book will help you as a Bible Believer to see that there is a Biblical mandate, regardless of media and international bias against the Jews who seek to have peace in their God-given homeland.

So, what is that Biblical mandate? Is the Bible clear about praying and blessing the Jews and the Land of Israel. We know God told Abraham that those that bless him and his descendants would be blessed. Yeshua taught a powerful parable that our Jewish Messianic guide, Andre taught us. (By the way, you don't want to go to Israel without connecting with Andre and his tour company KingSons Travel at www.kingsonstravel.com. Please don't use any one else but them, for they not only love the Lord, but have the most insight and revelation of anyone we have met in the Land. They will treat and protect you like family.)

Andre expounded this teaching of Yeshua first, while on a tour in Israel, but then he came to the United States and he taught our congregation as well. This totally rocked my world about praying and loving the Jewish people, and it also stirred our congregation because we never really saw this Scripture the way Andre does, primarily because he lives in the Land and understands the Bible from that perspective.

**Matthew 25:31-46** (TLV) "Now when the Son of Man comes in His glory, and all the angels with Him, then He will sit on His glorious throne. 32 All the nations will be gathered before Him, and He will separate them from one another, just as the shepherd separates the sheep from the goats. 33 And He will put the sheep on His right, but the goats on His left. 34 Then the King will say to those on His right, 'Come, you who are blessed by My Father, inherit the kingdom prepared for you from the foundation of the world. 35 For I was hungry and you gave Me something to eat; I was thirsty and you gave Me something to drink; I was a stranger and you invited Me in; 36 I was naked and you clothed Me; I was sick and you visited Me; I was in prison and you came to Me.' 37 "Then the righteous will answer Him, 'Lord, when did we see You hungry and feed You? Or thirsty and give You something to drink? 38 And when did we see You a stranger and invite You in? Or naked and clothe You? 39 When did we see You sick, or in prison, and come to You?' 40 "And answering, the King will say to them, 'Amen, I tell you, whatever you did to one of the least of these My brethren, you did it to Me.' 41 Then He will also say to those on the left, 'Go away from Me, you cursed ones, into the everlasting fire which has been prepared for the devil and his angels. 42 For I was hungry and you gave Me nothing to eat; I was thirsty and you gave Me nothing to drink; 43 I was a stranger and you did not invite Me in; naked and you did not clothe Me; sick and in prison and you did not visit Me.' 44 "Then they too will answer, saying, 'Lord, when did we see You hungry or thirsty or a stranger or

naked or sick or in prison, and did not care for You?'
45 Then He will answer them, saying, 'Amen, I tell you, whatever you did not do for one of the least of these, you did not do for Me.' 46 These shall go off to everlasting punishment, but the righteous into everlasting life."

This passage is very familiar. Many have heard that on Judgment Day there will be what are called "sheep" or "goat" nations. A "sheep nation" is one that supports Israel and blesses them. A "goat nation" is one that does not support or bless, but rather has disdain and might even try to harm them. We can see from Yeshua, that when He comes back to rule and reign on the earth, His throne will be set up in Jerusalem where He will reign as the King over the earth, fulfilling Zechariah's prophecy:

**Zechariah 14:9** (TLV) "And the LORD shall be king over all the earth: in that day shall there be one LORD, and his name one".

The Great Shepherd will separate those "sheep and goat nations," but you have to read the rest of the story to really understand why they are either a sheep or a goat. Yeshua basically said, "How you treat My brethren, the Jewish people, is really how you are treating Me, your Lord and Savior." Andre taught us that if we don't bless and pray for the Jewish people, it is a reflection on our treatment of Yeshua Himself. It was revelational! What if every Bible Believer got this revelation, too? In moments, the attitude of those Bible Believers would be known and exponentially change the political and cultural landscape. People everywhere would see "Christians" as the Jews' biggest supporters. They would be modeling this end-time teaching of "how you treat or bless a Jew is directly connected to your treatment of Yeshua, the coming King."

**Matthew 25:40 & 45** (TLV) 40 "And answering, the King will say to them, 'Amen, I tell you, **whatever you did to one of the least of these My brethren, you did it to Me.'** '
45 Then He will answer them, saying, 'Amen, I tell you, **whatever you did not do for one of the least of these, you did not do for Me.**

Think about how powerful it is to know every time you do something for a Jew, such as praying for them, loving them, helping them financially, you are doing it for Yeshua.
What a revelation, a mandate, a promise. It gives every Bible Believer the true and correct lens for understanding their role, especially in these last days. This is why we should be always praying, always loving and always supportive of the Jews and the Land of Israel. Yeshua taught us whatever we do for His brethren, the Jews, we do it for Him. Until Andre taught us this, we, like many of you, were taught that Yeshua was teaching about treating Believers well. Although we can extend this to Believers, the context of the teaching began with "sheep and goat nations" who would either be a blessing or a curse to Israel and the brethren of Yeshua, the Jews. Having this new understanding is key. When Yeshua was talking about His brethren, His audience got it. They understood that those nations who would not bless Israel on Judgment Day would go into everlasting judgment.

When Yeshua was on the earth, He taught many times about the fig tree. One of the understandings of the fig tree is that it represents the Land of Israel and its people. Look at this end-time teaching of Yeshua.

**Matthew 24:32-36** (TLV) "Now learn the parable from the fig tree. When its branch becomes tender and puts forth

leaves, you know that summer is near. 33 So also, when you see all these things, know that it is near, at the door.
34 Amen, I tell you, this generation will not pass away until all these things happen. 35 Heaven and earth will pass away, but My words will never pass away. 36 But of that day and hour no one knows, not even the angels of heaven nor the Son, except the Father alone.

The 24th chapter of Matthew is full of the end-time teachings of Yeshua. The people, like today, all wanted to know "When?" So, Yeshua told them to look at the fig tree. Most likely those that heard Him teach, knew, from the Scriptures and from the traditions past down to them, that the fig tree represented Israel. Yeshua says when the fig tree puts forth its leaves, that is when "summer" is near. The Greek word for "summer" can also be translated as "heat." So, in a sense, when these leaves appear, they are alerting to the nearness of the "heat" of summer. For those not familiar with the fig tree, when its leaves appear, they will also have new buds of fruit at the same time. If the fig tree has leaves, then it will have the seeds of fruit as well.

If we correctly discern the sign of the fig tree, then we know when the Land of Israel began to be restored as the homeland for the Jewish people in 1948, it was the beginning of this prophetic season we are in right now. After almost 2000 years, a nation was "born in a day." After the most horrific time of the Holocaust, the murdering of six million Jews, the Land of Israel was prophetically and powerfully restored.

**Isaiah 66:7-8** (TLV) Before she was in labor, she gave birth. Before her pain came, she delivered a male child. 8 Who has heard such a thing? Who has seen such things? Can a land be born in one day? Can a nation be brought forth at once? For as soon as Zion was in labor, she gave birth to her children.

Now that Israel has become a nation again, we are anticipating the "heat" of summer. The leaves, representing the land of Israel's covering and protection by the Lord, and the future harvest of the ripe figs is at hand. There is more about the fig tree in Scripture.

**Hosea 9:10** (TLV) "Like grapes in the wilderness I found Israel. Like early fruit on a fig tree in its first season I saw your fathers. They came to Baal-peor and devoted themselves to shame. So they became as detestable as the thing they loved.

**Proverbs 27:18** (NKJV) Whoever **keeps (H5341)** the fig tree will eat its fruit; So he who waits on his master will be honored.

**H5341 נָצַר nâtsar,** naw-tsar'; a primitive root; to guard, in a good sense (to protect, maintain, obey, etc.) or a bad one (to conceal, etc.):—besieged, hidden thing, keep(-er, -ing), monument, observe, preserve(-r), subtil, watcher(-man).

What does it mean to be a guarder or a watchman over the fig tree? Those who will watch and guard the fig tree will eat of its fruit. There also seems to be an honoring of the master for doing this.

If the fig tree is to be Israel and the Jewish people who have been given the Land, then who are to be the watchers on the wall? The Hebrew word Natsar נָצַר is telling us something that applies to all Believers, but especially those from the nations. We now have to dig this out a little to see where it takes us.

**Jeremiah 31:5-6** (TLV) For there will be a day when **watchmen** (H5341) will call out in the hill country of Ephraim, 'Arise, let us go up to Zion, to *Adonai* our God.'" 6 For thus says *Adonai*: "Sing aloud with joy for Jacob! Shout with the chief of the nations! Proclaim, give praise, and say: '*Adonai*, **save your people,** the remnant of Israel!'

Jeremiah talks about watchmen who will call out from Ephraim, the head of the northern Tribes that were scattered to the nations by the Assyrians in 722 BC. These lost and scattered Tribes, along with the nations, will say it is time to arise and go back to Zion, which is the Homeland of Israel, but also to Jerusalem, the place where the Lord's Temple stood. These watchmen seem to be from the nations, and with a great rejoicing, shout with those who are the Heads of Nations, and will join with Jacob giving great praises to the Lord. These watchmen continue to also ask for the Lord-YHVH to save His people, the remnant and residue of Israel. These watchmen are praying that the Jewish people see Yeshua, the only Savior of Israel. When Yeshua walked the earth, He came to seek after these Lost Sheep who had been scattered and swallowed up by the nations like Hosea had prophesied about. Now in the last days, it will be these who are coming home that will realize their Messianic mission of being the "watchmen on the wall" praying and standing with Jacob and the Jewish People.

This is such an amazing Scripture because it shows the role of nations in the last days. They are to call and join with Believers, Jews, and the native Israelites for a salvation from the Lord. The Scripture is pointing to a unison and communion between those from the nations and those who had been exiled from Ephraim, to now join back with Jacob with joy and praise. They are in agreement that God will save His people Israel. These watchmen are standing with

Israel and are part of the "sheep nations" that the Lord said they would do for the least of these My brethren.

Who are these watchman? I believe they are Believers like you who, now more than ever, know your mission is to ask God to save His beloved inheritance, the sheep who are lost or have been blinded to their Messiah.

If you put the English word for "Christian" in a translator like Google, and want to know what it would be in Hebrew, do you know what you would find? The Hebrew word for "watchman!"

Google Translate

English

christian

🔊                                                                    ▢

Hebrew

נוֹצְרִי

notzri

If you consider yourself a Bible-believing Christian, please don't delay any longer in your mission and mandate to pray and be the watchman on the wall for the Jewish people to know their Messiah. Pray for their protection from their many enemies who refuse to be a sheep and follow the Voice of the True Shepherd. The more Christians that get this message and begin to pray, the more spiritual strength will come to the Jewish people and the Land of Israel. Now that you know your role more fully, don't just call yourself a Christian any longer, call yourself a Watchmen, a guarder and protector of the Fig Tree. Summer and "heat" are at hand, but don't fear. God has a great harvest that you also will eat of, as long as you live your name!

**Jeremiah 31:6-12** (AMP) "For there will be a day when the **watchmen** On the hills of Ephraim cry out, 'Arise, and let us go up to Zion, To the Lord our God.'" 7 For thus says the Lord, "Sing aloud with gladness for Jacob, And shout for the first and foremost of the nations [the chosen people, Israel]; Proclaim, give praise and say, 'O Lord save Your people, The remnant of Israel!' 8 **"Behold, I am bringing them from the north country, And I will gather them from the remote parts of the earth**, Among them [will be] the blind and the lame, The woman with child and she who labors in childbirth, together; A great company, they will return here [to Jerusalem]. 9 "They will come with weeping [in repentance and for joy], And by [their] prayer [for the future] I will lead them; I will make them walk by streams of waters, On a straight path in which they will not stumble, For I am a Father to Israel, And Ephraim (Israel) is My firstborn." 10 Hear the word of the Lord, O you nations, And declare it in the isles and coastlands far away, And say, "**He who scattered Israel will gather him And will keep him as a shepherd keeps his flock.**" 11 For the Lord has ransomed Jacob And has redeemed him from the hand of him who was stronger than he. 12 "They will come and sing aloud and shout for joy on the height of Zion, And will be radiant [with joy] over the goodness of the Lord— For the grain, for the new wine, for the oil, And for the young of the flock and the herd. And their life will be like a watered garden, And they shall never sorrow or languish again.

# Chapter Four
## Group or Personal Study

1. If the fig tree represents Israel, could that be why Adam and Eve prophetically took the covering of the fig leaves to cover their nakedness?

_____
_____
_____
_____
_____

2. When Yeshua walked the earth, there was a time when Yeshua cursed the fig tree that only had leaves and no fruit. The disciples later saw that the fig tree quickly dried up from the roots and were amazed. Who do you think Yeshua was addressing or pointing to? Why did Yeshua expect to find fruit on the fig tree?

_____
_____
_____
_____
_____

3. According to the passage of Jeremiah, what are the watchmen supposed to be doing? Who are they supposed to be joining with?

_____
_____
_____
_____
_____

4. What does it mean to you to be a watchman on the wall? Are you willing to be counted as one that stands with the Jewish people and Israel in prayer?

5. What is the modern Hebrew equivalent for the *Natsar* watchman?

_____

_____

_____

_____

_____

6. How can we practically fulfill the mandate of Matthew 25? Are you doing the things Yeshua said to do to the least of Yeshua's brethren?

_____

_____

_____

_____

_____

7. Do you think the nation in which you were born or live in is a sheep or goat nation? Explain your thoughts.

_____

_____

_____

_____

_____

8. The Apostle Paul taught to pray without ceasing, and Yeshua said men ought always to pray. With the busyness of the modern way of life, how can we (you) find more time for prayer and intercession?

_____

_____

_____

_____

_____

9. Write down some of your favorite verses on the power of prayer.

_____

_____

# Chapter Five
## The Fulness of the Nations is Coming!

According to the Apostle Paul, there is coming a day called "the fulness of the nations." When this fulness comes, we can look forward to the greatest revival and awakening the world has ever seen. Before we look at the New Testament Scripture pertaining to this fulness, let's look at the Greek word for fulness, as well as the Hebrew cognate word so we can more "fully" understand the concept. First, look at its meaning in the dictionary.

**Fullness** (noun)
The state of being full, or of abounding; abundance; completeness.
Similar: abundance, completeness
Being full; completeness.
The degree to which a space is full.

*The GNU version of the Collaborative International Dictionary of English*

**G4138 Fulness: πλήρωμα plḗrōma**, play'-ro-mah; from G4137; repletion or completion, i.e. (subjectively) what fills (as contents, supplement, copiousness, multitude), or (objectively) what is filled (as container, performance, period):—which is put in to fill up, piece that filled up, fulfilling, full, fulness.

**G4137 πληρόω plēróō**, play-ro'-o; from G4134; to make replete, i.e. (literally) to cram (a net), level up (a hollow), or (figuratively) to furnish (or imbue, diffuse, influence), satisfy, execute (an office), finish (a period or task), verify (or coincide with a prediction), etc.:—accomplish, × after, (be) complete, end, expire, fill (up), fulfil, (be, make) full (come), fully preach, perfect, supply.

The Greek word for fulness is very similar to our American definition. It has to do with "fulfilling" and accomplishing a purpose and a full execution to completeness. If God has a plan for the Gentiles or nations as we will read about soon, then we must find out what that plan is. The fulfillment of this plan is a process, and we today are sovereignly being made aware of God's plan for the fulness of the nations. When we connect now to the Hebrew definition and look at the first mention of this word, you will see it connected to each creature's purpose and God-given design and blueprint. This word is also connected in the first mention to "blessing."

**H4390 Fill מָלֵא** mâlê', maw-lay'; or מָלָא mâlâ'; (Esther 7:5), a primitive root; to fill or (intransitively) be full of, in a wide application (literally and figuratively):—accomplish, confirm, consecrate, be at an end, be expired, be fenced, fill, fulfil, (be, become, × draw, give in, go) full(-ly, -ly set, tale), (over-) flow, fulness, furnish, gather (selves, together), presume, replenish, satisfy, set, space, take a (hand-) full, have wholly.

**Genesis 1:22 & 28** (TLV) Then God blessed them by saying, "Be fruitful and multiply and **fill (H4390)** the water in the seas. Let the flying creatures multiply on the land." 28 God blessed them and God said to them, "Be fruitful and multiply, **fill (H4390)** the land, and conquer it. Rule over the fish of the sea, the flying creatures of the sky, and over every animal that crawls on the land."

The Hebrew word for fulfillment in its first and second mentions are about the birds and the fish fulfilling their purpose of multiplication. The third mention is man fulfilling the same purpose with some added blessings of being fruitful, having dominion, and subduing. I like to think of this word as a way of describing a purpose, plan, and design realized and walked or fleshed out.

Let's read about this and see if we can do some more "spiritual mining."

**Romans 11:1-31** (TLV) I say then, God has not rejected His people, has He? May it never be! For I too am an Israelite, of the seed of Abraham, of the tribe of Benjamin. 2 God has not rejected His people whom He knew beforehand. Or do you not know what the Scripture says about Elijah, how he pleads with God against Israel? 3 "Adonai, they have killed your prophets, they have destroyed your altars; I alone am left, and they are seeking my life." 4 But what is the divine response to him? "I have kept for Myself seven thousand men who have not bowed the knee to Baal." 5 So in the same way also at this present time there has come to be a remnant according to God's gracious choice. 6 But if it is by grace, it is no longer by works; otherwise grace would no longer be grace. 7 What then? What Israel is seeking, it has not obtained; but the elect obtained it, and the rest were hardened— 8 just as it is written, "God gave them a spirit of stupor, eyes not to see and ears not to hear, until this very day." 9 And David says, "Let their table become a snare and a trap, a stumbling block and a retribution for them. 10 Let their eyes be darkened so they do not see, and bend their back continually." 11 I say then, they did not stumble so as to fall, did they? May it never be! But by their false step salvation has come to the Gentiles, to provoke Israel to jealousy. 12 Now if their transgression leads to riches for the world, and their loss riches for the Gentiles, then how much more their fullness! 13 **But I am speaking to you who are Gentiles.** Insofar as I am an emissary to the Gentiles, I spotlight my ministry 14 if somehow **I might provoke to jealousy my own flesh and blood and save some of them.** 15 For if their rejection leads to the reconciliation of the world, what will their acceptance be but life from the dead? 16 If the firstfruit is holy, so is the whole batch of dough; and if the root is holy, so are the branches. 17 But if some of the branches were broken off and you—being a wild olive—were grafted in among them and became a partaker of the root of the olive tree with its richness, 18 do not boast against the branches. But if you do boast, it is not you who support the root but the root supports you. 19 You will say then, "Branches were broken off so that I might be grafted in." 20 True enough. They were broken off because of unbelief, and you stand by faith. Do not be arrogant, but fear— 21 for if God did not spare the natural branches, neither will He spare you. 22 Notice then the kindness and severity of God: severity toward those who fell; but God's kindness toward you, if you continue in His kindness; otherwise you too will be cut off! 23 And they also, if they do not continue in their unbelief, will be grafted in; for God is able to graft them in again. 24 For if you were cut out of that which by nature is a wild olive tree, and grafted contrary to nature into a cultivated olive tree, how much more will these natural branches be grafted into their own olive tree? 25 For I do not want you, brothers and sisters, to be ignorant of this mystery—lest you be wise in your own eyes—that a partial hardening has come upon Israel until the fullness of the Gentiles has come in; 26 and in this way all Israel will be saved, as it is written, "The Deliverer shall come out of Zion. He shall turn away ungodliness from Jacob. 27 And this is My covenant with them, when I take away their sins." 28 Concerning the Good News, they are hostile for your sake; but concerning chosenness, they are loved on account of the fathers — 29 for the gifts and the calling of God are irrevocable. 30 For just as you once were disobedient to God but now have been shown mercy because of their disobedience, 31 in like manner these also have now been disobedient with the result that, because of the mercy shown to you, they also may receive mercy. 32 For God has shut up all in disobedience, so that He might show mercy to all.

So now we see it is God who will be working and blessing the Gentile nations to fulfill their purpose and plan to provoke Israel to jealousy. This, too, is prophesied by Moses himself in his speech before he dies. This provoking will continue to happen more and more as Bible Believers live more in line with the Kingdom culture that the Jewish people have been holding to and keeping from ancient times. This is why people all over the world are rediscovering the roots of their faith, and learning and teaching the Torah. Today many nations are living the fulness of their faith. They are learning, and yes, re-learning as a fulfillment of prophecy to provoke the Jew and awaken them to their Messiah and a renewal of their faith.

Now Romans 11 is a very lengthy passage and it will take a little work to begin to dig out some of its treasures. Back in the 8th chapter of Romans, we hear how God works all things to the good of those who love God and are called according to His purpose. Because God continues to work in good or bad situations, He, in His divine wisdom and plan, has a way of using even the wrong decisions we or His people Israel have made, to bring about a greater good. One thing you have to realize when we read this chapter, we have to understand who Paul is talking about when he speaks about Israel and what was their disobedience? Without the proper understanding, you might think he is talking about the Jewish people in general, and their fall from grace by not accepting Yeshua as the Messiah. Nowhere in this passage does Paul mention that rejection. He seems to be referring to some who were broken off because of unbelief, not because they rejected Yeshua. Paul was referring more to Israel's being in disobedience and constantly rebelling against what God had required of them.

If you know the history of Israel, then you know right after Solomon's reign, the Southern and Northern Kingdoms get divided and separate from one another. They will have different kings and through the Northern Kingdom's first king, Jeroboam, they will go into apostasy, idol worship, and an eventually will be conquered and scattered by the kingdom of Assyria. The Northern Kingdom became known as the House of Israel, while the Southern Kingdom was called Judah. The Northern Kingdom had 10 Tribes who were led by Ephraim, the son of Joseph who got a double portion blessing, prophetically given by his grandfather, Israel. As providence would have it, the Kingdom of Israel, as it was called, would be dismantled and the 10 Northern Tribes would be considered lost. Since God divorced these Tribes as stated in the book of Jeremiah, the only way these exiles could ever really come back to God and reconnect to the fig tree, Israel, would be when Messiah returns. One mystery of the Gospel is how Yeshua, through His death, burial, and resurrection, makes salvation and a born-again renewal to these Lost Tribes and sheep. Although we haven't seen all these Tribes come back physically to the Land yet, the way back has been established and a remnant of return has already begun. The fulness of the Gentiles, as Paul states, was a term mentioned much earlier in the Bible, back in the pronouncement of blessings over Ephraim and Manasseh in Genesis chapters 48 and 49. The blindness that has been over the Jewish people is only partial, and their eyes will be completely opened after the fulness of the Gentiles comes in. According to Apostle Paul's teachings, he wants to provoke to jealousy his own flesh and blood through these Gentiles that are now being restored back into their original inheritance. We might want to think of those who lost their birthright from the Northern Kingdom and their descendants as some sort of Hebrew Gentiles. They were, at one time, in covenant, but fell away and were cut off from the root like you see in Ezekiel 37.

**Ezekiel 37:11-14** (TLV) Then He said to me, "Son of man, these bones are the whole house of Israel. Behold, they say: 'Our bones are dried up; our hope is lost; we are cut off—by ourselves.' 12 Therefore prophesy and say to them, thus says *Adonai Elohim:* 'Behold, I will open your graves. I will bring you up out of your graves, My people. I will bring you back to the land of Israel. 13 You will know that I am *Adonai,* when I have opened your graves and brought you up out of your graves, My people. 14 I will put My *Ruach* in you and you will live. I will place you in your own land. Then you will know that I, *Adonai,* have spoken and that I have done it." It is a declaration of *Adonai.*

Ezekiel saw this great army awaken out of their graves. They were cut off, dry, dead, but the Spirit of the Lord breathes on them and they become alive again, BORN AGAIN! They were lost, but now they are found. The Lost Sheep not only return, but become a mighty army! They get rejoined, regrafted in again, to the household of faith, back to Abraham where they started. They return, all through the One true Messiah Yeshua. This is the mystery of the Good News! Even their fall from grace is turned out for the good of all who will now call on the name of the Lord and be saved. We know from the Scriptures that God's way is higher and His thoughts are also higher than ours. It is almost impossible for us to comprehend the riches of God's wisdom and grace. Even though the Northern Kingdom got dispersed and eventually swallowed up by the nations, it was all part of God's plan to bring about the greatest redemption and reversal that would begin to restore all mankind to their original state, back when the first man walked with the Lord in the Garden. Because of Yeshua, the WAY back to the Garden has already been opened. Although it is not the time for the "fulness" just yet, it has begun, and in one sense, like Yeshua said on the cross, "It is finished!"

**"Here now, but not yet!**

There is a term I learned studying the Hebrew and Jewish mindset: "Here now, but not yet!" This is why even though Yeshua made a way for the reconnection of those Lost Tribes and made a new connection with those from the nations, many modern Jews of today will deny Messiah Yeshua, because, "If He is the promised Messiah, then why hasn't He brought all the Tribes back to the Land? Where is the Messianic Kingdom?" This is another reason why all Believers, all true Christians should be praying that the eyes of the Jewish people would be opened and the stumbling blocks removed from them. Please pray, for they are your brothers and sisters. They are your family members. Pray that the veil be removed from their eyes and they would become part of the remnant and restoration of all things, even now, before the Lord comes back.

**Genesis 48:15-19** (TLV) Then he blessed Joseph and said, "The God before whom my fathers Abraham and Isaac walked, The God who has shepherded me throughout my life to this day, 16 The Angel who redeemed me from all evil, May He bless the boys, and may they be called by my name, and by the name of my fathers, Abraham and Isaac. May they multiply to a multitude in the midst of the land." 17 When Joseph saw that his father placed his right hand upon Ephraim's head, it was wrong in his eyes. So his took hold of his father's hand to remove it from Ephraim's head to Manasseh's head. 18 Joseph said to his father, "Not like that, my father, because this one's the firstborn. Put your right hand upon his head." 19 But his father refused and said, "I know, my son, I know. He also will become a people, and he also will become great. But his younger brother will become greater than he and **his seed will be the fullness of the nations**."

Ephraim's seed will become **"the fulness of the nations."** I want you to really think about that. The fulness of the nations was locked up in Ephraim, but was prophetically released when Israel put his hand on his head and prophesied this blessing onto him. In a sense, it was both a blessing and a curse. Because to get the blessing to the nations, Ephraim's seed would have to temporarily lose their connection to the covenant with the God of Israel. According to the book of Hosea, they would become a cake unturned, call the Torah a strange thing and swallowed by the nations. But if that didn't happen, then the nations whom they were now assimilated to would not have been able to be grafted into the rich roots and stock of Father Abraham. The Tribes of Ephraim and Manasseh are the sons of Joseph, but in the natural their mother was an Egyptian princess. They have mixed blood, yet are the perfect candidates for bringing all the nations, like a multitude of fish, into the Kingdom.

**Genesis 48:16** (CJB) the angel who has rescued me from all harm, bless these boys. May they remember who I am and what I stand for, and likewise my fathers Avraham and Yitz'chak, who they were and what they stood for. And may they grow into **teeming (fish)** multitudes on the earth."

To describe the blessing over Joseph's sons, he tells them they will **multiply like fish** on the earth. Now the last time I checked, fish are to live in the sea. Since fish multiply and spawn so rapidly as they move on the currents of the waters, we can see how this is a prophecy of the great future harvest of the nations, coming into and becoming a part of the family of Israel. There is much more here, especially once you realize that Ephraim and Manasseh were adopted by Jacob-Israel, and that adoption is what Paul uses to explain the nations coming to Messiah.

**Genesis 48:1-6** (TLV) After these things, someone told Joseph, "Behold, your father is sick." So he took his two sons, Manasseh and Ephraim, with him. 2 When someone told Jacob, saying, "Behold, your son Joseph has come to you," Israel summoned his strength and sat up in the bed. 3 Then Jacob said to Joseph, "El Shaddai appeared to me in Luz, in the land of Canaan, and blessed me." 4 He said to me, 'I am going to make you fruitful and multiply you and turn you into an assembly of peoples, and I will give this land to your seed after you as an everlasting possession.' 5 So now, your two sons, who were born to you in the land of Egypt before I came to you in Egypt, they are mine. Ephraim and Manasseh will be mine, just like Reuben and Simeon. 6 Any descendent of yours whom you father after them will be yours; they will be identified by the names of their brothers for their inheritance.

## These two sons are mine!

How powerful is this! The sons of Joseph get adopted into Israel. They are going to get some type of first-born blessing, the way Reuben was to receive as the natural firstborn. The mystery and blessings of adoption is something I talk about in my book "Hacked." Children who are adopted understand that they are chosen and loved by their parents. When this is carried out in the New Testament, it is to be understood with the adoption of Ephraim and Manasseh because they are the seed and the prophetic picture of adoption.

**Romans 8:15-16** (TLV) For you did not receive the spirit of slavery to fall again into fear; rather, you received the Spirit of adoption, by whom we cry, "*Abba*! Father!" 16 The *Ruach* Himself bears witness with our spirit that we are children of God.

**Romans 9:3-5** (TLV) For I would pray that I myself were cursed, banished from Messiah for the sake of my people— my own flesh and blood, 4 who are Israelites. **To them belong the adoption** and the glory and the covenants and the giving of the *Torah* and the Temple service and the promises. 5 To them belong the patriarchs—and from them, according to the flesh, the Messiah, who is over all, God, blessed forever. Amen.

When you read the Bible and understand it is seamless from beginning to the end and you begin to connect and sew together all the threads, the tapestry of the Gospel gets clearer.

The fulness of the nations was promised to the descendants or seed of Ephraim. What a powerful promise. We see Paul connecting to that promise in Romans chapter 11. I can't imagine how Paul must have felt as the first person to dig these truths out. He was sharing the mystery of the Gospel that had been hidden, but was being revealed in the last days.

Today, we too are seeing more unveiling, and we are increasing with spiritual revelational knowledge as promised in the book of Daniel.

**Daniel 12:1-4** (AMP) "Now at that [end] time Michael, the great [angelic] prince who stands guard over the children of your people, will arise. And there will be a time of distress such as never occurred since there was a nation until that time; but at that time your people, everyone who is found written in the Book [of Life], will be rescued. 2 Many of those who sleep in the dust of the ground will awake (resurrect), these to everlasting life, but some to disgrace and everlasting contempt (abhorrence). 3 Those who are [spiritually] wise will shine brightly like the brightness of the expanse of heaven, and those who lead many to righteousness, [will shine] like the stars forever and ever. 4 But as for you, Daniel, conceal these words and seal up the scroll until the end of time. Many will go back and forth and search anxiously [through the scroll], and knowledge [of the purpose of God as revealed by His prophets] will [greatly] increase.

As the spiritual knowledge of God is increasing and being made available to the nations, please recognize you are living in prophecy fulfilled right now. The nations are being awakened to their fulness, the provoking to jealousy is happening, and now is the time to pray and love the Jewish people like you never have before. The more you pray and the more you bless, the more you will see God's hand working through you. The prayers of the righteous avail much! Every true Believer will be awakened to this biblical mandate.

## Chapter Five
### Group or Personal Study

1. What does the word "fulness" mean according to the dictionary?

_____

_____

_____

_____

_____

2. What does the word "fulness" mean in the Greek and Hebrew?

_____

_____

_____

_____

_____

3. What does the first mention of the word "fulness" have to do with?

_____

_____

_____

_____

_____

4. What are some ways you as a Believer can provoke Israel to jealousy?

_____

_____

_____

_____

_____

5. The multiplication and blessing over Joseph's sons are likened to _____.

6. Which son of Joseph gets the blessing of fruitfulness?

_____
_____
_____
_____
_____

7. What does the adoption of Ephraim and Manasseh point to in the New Testament?

_____
_____
_____
_____
_____

8. What does the crossing of Jacob's hands in that blessing, hint to?

_____
_____
_____
_____
_____

9. What Scripture in the book of Acts connects to the prophecy of Daniel that says spiritual knowledge will increase?

_____
_____
_____
_____
_____

10. Can you describe any signs of the fulness of the nations coming in your family or congregation?

_____
_____
_____
_____
_____

# Chapter Six
## Tying It All Together

When I began thinking about writing this book, I wanted to make sure it got to the right audience. The Lord taught about casting pearls before swine. Of course, when anyone seeking truth finds Messiah, I, along with the angels, rejoice. For the most part, those who are the haters of Israel will not be easily swayed or gently nudged away from their deeply held beliefs. Even if you have all your ducks in a row and facts clearly laid out with positive proof, it will not be received. Cognitive Dissonance will keep the unbelievers in unbelief. There is a saying in Jewish thought that "If you are a Believer in the Lord, no proof is necessary, and if you are not a Believer in the Lord, no proof will ever be sufficient." I wish that statement didn't pan out, but as I have been awakened, along with many others, to the truth of this book, there are also many who, no matter what, will not be on the right side of this issue. The right side being a love for Israel and wanting to bless and pray for the Jewish people. To also support them with our prayers, generous resources and words. For those who are on the fence about this, I believe only the Lord can convince someone and make clear the mission and mandate of Believers concerning the Land of Israel and the Jewish people today. I now want to attempt to see if we can continue to thread these thoughts together biblically. The Tabernacle of David, according to the book of Acts, is when the nations seek the God of Israel.

**Acts 15:12-21** (TLV) Then the whole group became silent and were listening to Barnabas and Paul as they were describing in detail all the signs and wonders God had done through them among the Gentiles. 13 After they finished speaking, Jacob answered, "Brothers, listen to me. 14 Simon has described how God first showed His concern by taking from the Gentiles a people for His Name. 15 The words of the Prophets agree, as it is written: 16 'After this I will return and rebuild the fallen **tabernacle of David**. I will rebuild its ruins and I will restore it, 17 so that the rest of humanity may seek the Lord— namely **all the Gentiles** who are called by My name— says Adonai, who makes these things 18 known from of old.19 ' Therefore, I judge not to trouble those from among the Gentiles who are turning to God— 20 but to write to them to abstain from the contamination of idols, and from sexual immorality, and from what is strangled, and from blood. 21 For Moses from ancient generations has had in every city those who proclaim him, since he is read in all the synagogues every Shabbat."

The prophecy of the Gentiles represents the nations who will come under the same tabernacle as Israel. This is a direct quote from the book of Amos chapter 9. The nations will see Adonai and they will begin to learn His Ways. Isaiah 60 says that the nations will come to the Light of Israel, for their mission is to be a Light to all the Nations. This is why God chose Israel, not because they were the best or the largest, they were and still are small. God chose Israel because He knew they would say yes and do and hear the Torah and share it with the nations. The Lord's plan of salvation from the fall in the Garden, to the New Jerusalem coming down in the book of Revelation was for all people to know the True God who created the Heavens and the Earth. God, in His sovereignty, chose a man by the name of Abraham to this great task. He is called the Father of Faith to all who believe, including the Believers we read about in the book of Acts and the New Testament. The same seamless Gospel was prophesied by God Himself.

**Genesis 3:15** (CJB) I will put animosity between you and the woman, and between your descendant and her descendant; he will bruise your head, and you will bruise his heel."

The crushing or bruising of the serpent was accomplished through the seed of the woman. The woman represents Israel and the Jewish people. It is through their seed, specifically the Seed that came from Abraham, Isaac, Jacob, Judah, and later through David and through Miriam (Mary), that brought Messiah into the world to seek and to save that which was lost. A final redemption and reversal have begun; yes, it is here now, but not yet. You can choose to be a part of God's army of spiritual warriors who choose to honor what God says to honor.

**Isaiah 9:5-6** (TLV) For to us a child is born, a son will be given to us, and the government will be upon His shoulder. His Name will be called Wonderful Counselor, Mighty God My Father of Eternity, Prince of Peace. 6 Of the increase of His government and *shalom* there will be no end— on the throne of David and over His kingdom— to establish it and uphold it through justice and righteousness from now until forevermore. The zeal of *Adonai-Tzva'ot* will accomplish this.

Through the seed of the woman, the seed of Abraham, and the seed of the Jewish people, the entire world receives the that blessing promised to Abraham. This is the blessing; that through Abraham all the families of the earth will be blessed. Those that bless Abraham and his seed will be blessed, for they will be the sheep nations. Those who curse, make light of, or dishonor them will be dishonored as a goat nation. I hope you as a Bible Believer are getting stronger and stronger in the Lord as you make a commitment to stand with, bless, and pray for the Jewish people and the Promised Land called Israel.

We hope every reader of this book will have the ammunition through the Scriptures, with a holy boldness birthed out of a love for God, to love the Jewish people.

**2 Chronicles 20:7** (AMP) O our God, did You not drive out the inhabitants of this land before Your people Israel and give it forever to the descendants of Your friend Abraham?

We know that Abraham is called the "friend of God' or "one who loves God." Because of God's unconditional love and promise to that divinely chosen man, even today, Abraham's descendants, given through the miracle child Isaac, still have the biblically legal and God-given rights to live peacefully in the Land without fear of other nations trying to divide it among its inhabitants.

Abraham, the first Hebrew, purchased in Hebron a field and cave to bury his wife, Sarah. It is where all the Patriarchs are buried today. No one can dispute this land sale. Abraham was told by God to lift up his eyes and look in all four directions, to walk the length and breadth of the Land, for it was his by promise, and deeded by God Himself to the descendants of Abraham, the Jewish people of today.

God promised Abraham two specific but related things. God promised Abraham children and land. Abraham lived his entire life to make a name for God in the earth. He understood that somehow that Land and those children would be a way to exalt the name of the Lord to all other nations of the earth.

**Hebrews 11:8-12** (Amp) 8 By faith Abraham, when he was called [by God], obeyed by going to a place which he was to receive as an inheritance; and he went, not knowing where he was going. 9 By faith he lived as a foreigner in the promised land, as in a strange land, living in tents [as nomads] with Isaac and Jacob, who were fellow heirs of the same promise. 10 For he was [waiting expectantly and confidently] looking forward to the city which has foundations, [an eternal, heavenly city] whose architect and builder is God. 11 By faith even Sarah herself received the ability to conceive [a child], even [when she was long] past the normal age for it, because she considered Him who had given her the promise to be reliable and true [to His word]. 12 So from one man, though he was [physically] as good as dead, were born as many descendants as the stars of heaven in number, and innumerable as the sand on the seashore.

**Galatians 3:29** (CJB) Also, if you belong to the Messiah, you are seed of Avraham and heirs according to the promise.

You are an heir of the promises of Abraham. What has been given to Israel and the Jewish people, you are now connected with them. You are a fellow-heir of these promises. This does not negate or replace those given these promises who have or can trace their natural bloodline as a physical descendant of Abraham. Since you are now part of that great family, isn't it time for you to embrace your spiritual roots and DNA? As the Lord draws closer to us in these last days, more and more people will be awakened to their true spiritual identity. Those who are born Jewish will be awakened to their Messiah from the Tribe of Judah. Those who are from the seed of Ishmael will begin to honor the God of his father, Abraham. Those Bible-believing Christians from the nations will begin to make a positive and prolific stand with Israel. All those connected to Abraham will arise and defend the Jewish people and support the Land of Israel. A Remnant is beginning to arise and I believe you are a part of what God is still requiring.

**Micah 6:8** (TLV) He has told you, humanity, what is good, and what *Adonai* is seeking from you: Only to practice justice, to love mercy, and to walk humbly with your God.

It is going to take a humble people to embrace the mission and mandate to stand unashamedly alongside of the Jews. There is so much negativity and false propaganda that many of the elect have already fallen prey to the lies of the enemy. Our young people have to be especially educated on which side to stand. The culture will eat truth for lunch, breakfast, and dinner, too! The power of culture to assimilate the masses into false belief systems and the counterfeit life cannot be undersold. Please do not discount the culture's influence over your beliefs and your children's beliefs. Everywhere you go, and almost everything you see or listen to has been influenced by the culture of the nations. The only way to combat that is to come out from among them and separate yourself. This is no easy task. Alexander the Great, when he conquered new territory and land, would bring the Greek culture immediately into every way of life of these newly assimilated lands. Once the Greek culture was injected into every facet of life, it spread and became the new normal. This is exactly what happened to the Jewish people in the story of Hanukkah, and if you read about it, you will find many of the Jews ended up bowing down and losing their true identity because the culture swallowed them up.

When you associate yourself with the Jewish people, get ready to be persecuted, maligned, misunderstood, and lied on!


**Matthew 5:10-12** (TLV) "Blessed are those who have been persecuted for the sake of righteousness, for theirs is the kingdom of heaven. 11 "Blessed are you when people revile you and persecute you and say all kinds of evil against you falsely, on account of Me. 12 Rejoice and be glad, for your reward in heaven is great! For in the same way they persecuted the prophets who were before you."

Persecution happened throughout the book of Acts, but the persecution did not stop the Gospel, it propelled it. The more you or I align with the Jewish people and the Land of Israel we can expect more persecuting, but along with it will be the greatest harvest into the Kingdom any generation has seen. Please don't back down when you feel the heat, for a great multitude of fish is on the way. An abundance of fish, large and small are coming into the Kingdom of God and they will be joined to the Jewish people and to the Land of Israel. They will love the Jew, and they will not be afraid to identify themselves with their spiritual heritage. The persecution is a way for God to nudge Believers to do what they should have been doing the whole time. When we get too comfortable in Egypt or Sodom, God sometimes uses persecution to wake us out of our slumber.

**Matthew 13:21** (NKJV) yet he has no root in himself, but endures only for a while. For when **tribulation** or **persecution** arises because of the word, immediately he stumbles.

According to Yeshua's teaching of the Parable of the Sower, He connects the trials of tribulation and persecution coming because of the Word. The Lord wants the Word that is in you to come through you to demonstrate the Light and Life of the Kingdom. Every time someone receives the Word, in some way they will now be tested and persecuted because they said yes to the Word. Saying yes to the Word is the beginning of persecutions. Those who say yes, might not get "liked" by the culture. Instead, those receiving God's Word, loving the Jews, and standing and supporting the Land of Israel will be on the side of persecutions.

A man who is Jewish once told me to tell the Christians that if they come on the side of the Jews, they better get ready for a lot of trouble and persecution. He said, "Why would you Christians want to come over to our side? For on your side everything is cool and everyone likes you. If you identify with us, you are positioning yourself to be hated many times for no reason other than being Jewish." This same man told his Jewish son, "It is way easier to be a Christian than a Jew." Those who are born Jewish or begin to align and identify with them will be persecuted along with them.

**Mark 4:16-19** (AMP) In a similar way these [in the second group] are the ones on whom seed was sown on rocky ground, who, when they hear the word, immediately receive it with joy [but accept it only superficially]; 17 and they have no real root in themselves, so they endure only for a little while; then, when **trouble or persecution comes because of the word,** immediately they [are offended and displeased at being associated with Me and] stumble *and* fall away. 18 And others are the ones on whom seed was sown among the thorns; these are the ones who have heard the word, 19 but the worries *and* cares of the world [the distractions of this age with its worldly pleasures], and the deceitfulness [and the false security or glamour] of wealth [or fame], and the passionate desires for all the other things creep in and choke out the word, and it becomes unfruitful.

I believe God is calling the Bible-believing Christians to make their stand, even in the face of persecution and troubles. Identifying with Messiah will mean the eventual coming out of the comforts of the Babylonian system of compromise and mixture with the world. God specifically told His people Israel they were to be distinctly His.

**Leviticus 18:2-5** (AMP) ""Speak to the children of Israel and say to them, 'I am the Lord your God. 3 You shall not do what is done in the land of Egypt where you lived, and you shall not do what is done in the land of Canaan where I am bringing you. You shall not follow their statutes (practices, customs). 4 You are to follow My judgments (precepts, ordinances) and keep My statutes and live by them. I am the Lord your God. 5 So you shall keep My statutes and My judgments, by which, if a person keeps them, he shall live; I am the Lord."

The realm of Egypt represents our life in bondage under sin. Before receiving Messiah, we were locked in a prison of sin and death. Satan, like Pharaoh, is a cruel taskmaster. He did not want to let you go, but thankfully you were delivered from that dark place and translated into the Kingdom of the Son. The realm where the Canaanites lived before they were dispossessed by Israel represents way the enemy traffics the souls of men and makes us merchandise. This was the spirit of Nimrod who hunted for these souls. Satan, too, is about trafficking and trading and he wants to use humanity for his own evil purposes, leaving mankind defiled and deceived in the process.

When the beloved John wrote, it was from the perspective of intimacy with God. He put his head on the breast and heart of Yeshua and he heard His heartbeat. Are you willing to disconnect from this world's beastly system? Are you willing to stand and pray for the Jewish people and the Land of Israel?

**1 John 2:15-17** (TLV) Do not love the world or the things in the world. If anyone loves the world, the love of the Father is not in him. 16 For everything in the world—the desire of the flesh, the desire of the eyes, and the boasting of life—is not from the Father but from the world. 17 The world is passing away along with its desire, but the one who does the will of God abides forever.

God is calling us, even now, out of Babylon because in the end, she is "Fallen, fallen." Those who stay in her beastly and seductive system will eventually be destroyed with her.

Because Messiah has not set up the physical Kingdom yet, we have to deal with the many "lies" and "deceptions" that flood and bombard us daily. The war in Gaza has been a hot topic and the horrors that our Jewish brothers and sisters in the Land of Israel have gone through since October 7, 2023 will never be fully realized. We must never forget. We must remember, not only what was done, but to pray and stand with them in their sufferings, as well as their triumphs.

I highly suggest that you limit your viewing of news and social media, and focus more of your quest for truth, insight and knowledge through prayer and the continued study of God's Word. If you feel you cannot completely give them up, then I would suggest finding sources that are more connected to the Jewish people and the Land of Israel. My wife and I have many personal friends and connections in the Land, and because of they have "boots on the ground", we hear from a perspective that is not usually shown on the traditional media outlets.

Because the enemy knows that if you tout a lie long enough repetitively and also make the lie bigger and greater than one can imagine, eventually the masses will believe the lie. Today it is harder than ever for the average person, even Believers, to discern right from wrong and good from evil. The lines have been intentionally blurred and the standard of truth has been long forgotten. The generations before us have no real foundation of Bible Truth and many in the older generations have not been taught correctly in regards to the Jews and the Land of Israel. Yeshua said in the last days that even the elect would be deceived. I like to think of our generation as "Torah-less." The foundation of the Bible starting with the first five books have been skipped over today and many have been told to disconnect from it because it is irrelevant. We must have more Bible-believing people, starting with pastors and leaders, getting back to the biblical foundation of faith in the God of Israel. Without going back to the timeless and true Scriptural foundations, "What can the righteous do?"

A spiritual revolution can start with you and me. We must be willing to pay the price, to be laughed at, misunderstood, persecuted, reproached, and even ostracized by our own friends and camps. God might allow some of you to use your influence to bring many out of the Babylonian systems and into the Way of the Messiah. I pray God would give you the platform to demonstrate a love for the Jewish people and the Land of Israel, and bring many "fish," large and small, into this boat.

One of the misunderstood terms is the name that was given to the Land of Israel by the Romans. There are many articles written about this divisive term. I will put a few links for you to read at the end of this chapter.

[5]*The ancient Romans pinned the name on the Land of Israel. In 135 CE, after stamping out the province of Judea's second insurrection, the Romans renamed the province Syria Palaestina—that is, "Palestinian Syria." They did so resentfully, as a punishment, to obliterate the link between the Jews (in Hebrew, Y'hudim and in Latin Judaei) and the province (the Hebrew name of which was Y'hudah). "Palaestina" referred to the Philistines, whose home base had been on the Mediterranean coast.*

It has been very unfortunate that this name, "Palestine" in our modern times, has been commonly understood by the masses as the Land of Israel and the home of the

———————————

5 https://mosaicmagazine.com/observation/israel-zionism/
2021/12/the-forgotten-history-of-the-term-palestine/

"Palestinian" people. Once you research this subject and term, you will see how this name has been hijacked, or what one writer says, "amputated" and used as a tactic to cause the masses to believe one of the enemy's greatest and most outlandish lies.

The Land of Israel was given to Abraham and his seed by a Covenant of Salt. For over 3500 years the Jewish people have lived in the Land. There are biblical and historical records that prove them to be the people who have the rights to this special Land. Because many of you reading this book have already bought the "lie" and "have the t-shirt," it will be challenging for you now to discern the truth on this issue.

Once a name is attached to something, it brings with it a fame, a reputation, and a history of deeds. The term Palestine or Palestinian has been propagated to the world as a peaceful and loving people who are being taken advantage of by the mean bully nation of Israel and the Jews. This cannot be further from the truth.

I have been to Israel many times, and the Jewish authorities have already allowed the many Arab cities autonomy and the Jewish people cannot even go in to those places. Many of these Arabs love the Jewish people and are blessed because they work in the Land of Israel and are paid very well. They are not abused or mistreated in any way. Many of them live in very large houses and their communities lack nothing at all because Israel allows them to settle and live peacefully in their Land. Unfortunate is how these Arabs are taken advantage of by their own leaders; leaders whom they elected, that have been in power for years.

When we go to Israel, we have been with the Arabs, and our tour company always has an amazing Arab driver who looks out for us on our travels. We don't want to beat up or malign all the Arabs and those who call themselves Palestinians, because they too are caught between a rock and a hard place. We must pray for them when we pray for Israel. Many of these Arabs are descendants of Ishmael, Abraham's son by Hagar. We must pray that their eyes, too, are opened to the true Messiah and they can reconnect to their roots through Messiah Yeshua.

I believe God can work mightily, even through the trials and tribulations of the War in Gaza, to bring about a true restoration between the sons of Ishmael and the sons of Isaac. This is another reason why we must stand with the Jews and also pray for the Peace of Jerusalem and the Land of Israel.

As we get closer to the future of the Messianic Kingdom and the 1000-year reign of Messiah, the birth pangs will get closer and increase with intensity. This is the time to have the strength to birth what God has designed and planned.

Please do not draw back your faith now! You will not be ashamed or disappointed as you continue to align yourself now with the Jewish people in your prayers and support. This is not a time to live in fear, but rather to be resolved and more committed to the faith and the scriptural mandates in the Bible.

Remember, because of Yeshua you have been grafted into the Covenant. You are an heir with the Jewish people to all God promised to Abraham and to his seed. The foundations of the faith run deep and are very strong. As long as you build on that "Rock," whatever storms may rage will not cause the House of Israel to fall.


**Matthew 7:21- 27** (TLV) "Not everyone who says to Me, 'Lord, Lord!' will enter the kingdom of heaven, but he who does the will of My Father in heaven. 22 Many will say to Me on that day, 'Lord, Lord, didn't we prophesy in Your name, and drive out demons in Your name, and perform many miracles in Your name?' 23 Then I will declare to them, 'I never knew you. Get away from Me, you workers of lawlessness! (*Torah-lessness*)'" 24 "Therefore everyone who hears these words of Mine and does them will be like a wise man who built his house on the rock. 25 And the rain fell, and the floods came, and the winds blew and beat against that house; and yet it did not fall, for its foundation had been built on the rock. 26 Everyone who hears these words of Mine and does not act on them will be like a foolish man who built his house on the sand. 27 And the rain fell, and the floods came, and the winds blew and beat against that house; and it fell—and great was its fall."

It is my prayer that this book has begun to open your eyes and reconnect you to your spiritual roots as a Bible Believer. If you are a pastor or a leader in a congregation, you have more responsibility now that you know the truth. Ask God to open doors and to prepare the hearts of the people to receive as you share in love and with respect with those who might not have heard or been open to the message of loving and standing with the Jewish people. Pray that God leads you to those whose hearts and minds are ready to receive the Word.

**James 1:19-27** (TLV) Know this, my dear brothers and sisters: let every person be quick to listen, slow to speak, and slow to anger — 20 for human anger doesn't produce the righteousness of God. 21 So put away all moral filth and excess of evil and receive with humility the implanted word, which is able to save your souls. 22 But be doers of the word, and not hearers only, deluding yourselves. 23 For if anyone is a hearer of the word and not a doer, he is like a man who looks at his natural face in a mirror— 24 for once he looks at himself and goes away, he immediately forgets what sort of person he was. 25 But the one who looks intently into the perfect Torah, the Torah that gives freedom, and continues in it, not becoming a hearer who forgets but a doer who acts—he shall be blessed in what he does. 26 If anyone thinks he is religious and yet does not bridle his tongue but deceives his heart, this person's religion is futile. 27 Pure and undefiled religion before our God and Father is this: to care for orphans and widows in their distress, and to keep oneself unstained by the world.

Links for additional references to Palestine:

https://www.youtube.com/watch?v=3VKlTuDch48

https://blogs.timesofisrael.com/the-origin-and-appropriation-of-the-word-palestine-may-surprise-you/

https://mosaicmagazine.com/observation/israel-zionism/2021/12/the-forgotten-history-of-the-term-palestine/

https://www.jewishvirtuallibrary.org/origin-of-quot-palestine-quot

# Chapter Six:
## Group or Personal Study

1. Who is the Tabernacle of David for?

_____

_____

_____

_____

_____

2. According to Isaiah chapter 60, what is Israel's mission? Please read and write down that verse, and other verses in the Bible that confirm that mission.

_____

_____

_____

_____

_____

3. What are the two specific things God promised to Abraham?

_____

_____

_____

_____

_____

4. Through the seed of the_____, the seed of _____ and the seed of the _____, the entire world gets the very blessing promised to Abraham.

5. According to Leviticus 18 and 1 John chapter 5, what are we who identify with Israel not to become? How does this apply to you and your family?

_____
_____
_____
_____
_____

6. What can you implement in your life or family to separate yourself from the culture of the world?

_____
_____
_____
_____
_____

7. What realm does Egypt represent?

_____
_____
_____
_____
_____

8. What does the Canaanite represent?

_____
_____
_____
_____
_____

9. According to the Parable of the Sower, what brings tribulation and persecution?

_____
_____
_____
_____

10. Who introduced the name Palestine and why?

_____

_____

_____

_____

_____

11. What does the name Palestine really mean and where does it come from? After reading the articles and listening to the YouTube link, what are your thoughts about this term?

_____

_____

_____

_____

_____

# Chapter 7
## The Kingdom Way to Pray

In this chapter our goal is to stir you, the reader, to pray for the Jewish people and the Land of Israel. Your prayers can make a difference. God's chosen remnant, the Jewish people, have a long history of prayer, starting with the very first intercessor Father Abraham. He was a man of prayer, but so was Daniel, David, Samuel and many more Jews including our Messiah Yeshua. Prayer is a form of worship as well as studying the Word.

God can give you a grace to pray. When that happens, your prayers will be ignited and infused with power through the Holy Spirit. Many Orthodox Jews pray three times a day. They have a morning, afternoon, and evening prayer time and start and end each day with the "Shema." The basis for the three times a day is found in the book of Daniel. It seems the three times a day most likely also connected the people to the three times of day the offerings were offered when the Tabernacle or Temple stood. These were the morning, afternoon, and evening sacrifices that were offered on the altar, drawing the nations closer to God.

**Daniel 6:10-11** (AMP) Now when Daniel knew that the document was signed, he went into his house (now in his roof chamber his windows were open toward Jerusalem); he continued to get down on his knees three times a day, praying and giving thanks before his God, as he had been doing previously. 11 Then, by agreement, these men came [together] and found Daniel praying and making requests before his God.

**Mark 12:28-31** (TLV) One of the Torah scholars came and heard them debating. Seeing that Yeshua had answered them well, he asked Him, "Which commandment is first of all? 29 Yeshua answered, "The first is, 'Shema Yisrael, Adonai Eloheinu, Adonai echad. Hear, O Israel, the Lord our God, the Lord is One. 30 And you shall love Adonai your God with all your heart, and with all your soul, and with all your mind, and with all your strength.' 31 The second is this, 'You shall love your neighbor as yourself.' There is no other commandment greater than these."

We know Yeshua taught that the Shema was at the very beginning of the greatest commandment of loving God with your all, (and the second, loving your neighbor as yourself). The Hebrew word Shema, is more accurately translated as "to listen, follow, hear and obey." Praying the Shema is a call for Israel and the Jewish people to hear and obey the Lord their God.

Yeshua Himself said to seek first the Kingdom and the righteousness that God requires. A tradition of praying the Shema twice a day is a way a Jew practically fulfills the command to think and talk about God "when your rise up and when you lie down" like it says in Deuteronomy chapter 6.

**Deuteronomy 6:4-9** (TLV) "Hear O Israel, the Lord our God, the Lord is one. 5 Love Adonai your God with all your heart and with all your soul and with all your strength. 6 These words, which I am commanding you today, are to be on your heart. 7 You are to teach them diligently to your children, and speak of them when you sit in your house, when you walk by the way, when you lie down and when you rise up. 8 Bind them as a sign on your hand, they are to be as frontlets between your eyes, 9 and write them on the doorposts of your house and on your gates.

The mandate to pray and stand for the Jewish people and the Land of Israel is something I hope you will now begin to do, and if you have been doing it already, may you do it with a greater urgency and fervor.

When Yeshua Messiah was on the earth, the disciples saw the evidence of the Lord's prayer life that propelled and undergirded His mighty ministry. The disciples plainly asked the Lord to teach them to pray like He did, for when Yeshua asked and prayed, miracles abounded.  This is not to say that miracles and healings always abounded, for when the people failed to honor Yeshua as Messiah, the Lord Himself could not do many mighty works in His home city. The power of honor is a key component in God's Kingdom culture, but few have connected it to prayer and to the prayers of Yeshua and the Jewish people.

The Apostle Paul seemed to be very big on prayer as well. He told us to "pray without ceasing." Paul taught his young mentee, Timothy, to pray starting with "all men" that they might be saved. In the book of Ephesians, Paul teaches and expounds on prayer saying he does not cease to pray for the people he is writing to.

The Apostle Paul grew up as a scholar and learned to pray in the school of Gamaliel his "Rabbi-Teacher." The Jews of his day were used to fasting twice a week and praying as a way of life. It is hard for those of us today to really connect to what was normal life for any religious Jew or follower of Messiah back in the first century, the time of Yeshua and the book of Acts. Even though you and I can't completely relate to the culture of prayer during those days, it can motivate you take up a new mantle of prayer and build upon those firm foundations. We know prayer is important to Yeshua, His disciples, the Apostles, and the followers of Messiah in the book of Acts. Now it's time to make prayer a priority, for it is a spiritual portal and door to bringing heaven to earth.

**Luke 11:1-6** (TLV) Now Yeshua was praying in a certain place. When He finished, one of His disciples said to Him, "Master, teach us to pray, just as John taught his disciples." 2 Then Yeshua said to them, "When you pray, say, 'Father, sanctified be Your Name, Your kingdom come. 3 Give us each day our daily bread. 4 And forgive us our sins, for we also forgive everyone indebted to us. And lead us not into temptation."

Yeshua understood the power of prayer and gave His disciples a template that has been built upon as a way to approach God's throne and to establish God's kingdom and will upon the earth. The power of prayer is in your arsenal, but you must take the arrow of prayer out of the quiver and begin to use it to put the enemy in check. As you can see from Yeshua's and Daniel's prayers, they always start praying with giving God either thanksgiving or praise. There is much biblical reference for this. Praise and thanksgiving are a way to enter the throne of heaven.

If you are a Believer in Messiah, then you know because of the work of Messiah, you can also come to that heavenly throne in boldness, looking to receive the grace and mercy you need. After we have honored our God through offering our worship and praise with thanksgiving, then we can approach the throne through the work of Yeshua's atoning blood and ask Him for mercy and grace upon Israel, His beloved people. There are Jewish prayers that go back hundreds and thousands of years that also pull-on God's grace and mercy. The Jewish prayers are usually all based on Scripture and filled with direct quotes, so when these prayers are prayed, they are reminding God of His covenant and Word. There are so many promises about the restoration of Israel to their land and the eternal covenant blessing promised the Jewish people. God's promises are without repentance and He will not forsake His people, ever! This is why, even the more, we need to pray God's Kingdom and will be done over them. We can speak, declare, and pray the promises back to God. The Scripture declares for us all to "Seek the Lord while He may be found and call upon Him while He is near." (Isaiah 55:6)

The Amidah, known also as the Standing Prayer, is a prayer that is prayed three times a day. Here is a short summary of that prayer template so you can see that the Jewish model of prayer is very Kingdom oriented.

**Summary of the Amidah Prayer:**

**1. The First Blessing: Fathers ("Avot")**
My God, open my lips, and my mouth will speak Your praises. Blessed are You Adonai, our God, and God of our ancestors, God of Abraham, God of Isaac and God of Jacob. The great, the mighty and the awesome God who bestows lovingkindness, Creator of all. God recalls the kindness of our ancestors and will bring the redeemer to their children's children, for God's name's sake, with love. Sovereign, helper, savior and shield.  Blessed are You Adonai, Shield of Abraham.

**2. The Second Blessing: Powers ("Gevurot")**
You are mighty forever, Adonai, You give life to the dead – great is Your saving power (summer) Who causes the dew to fall (winter) Who causes the winds to blow and the rain to fall. You sustain the living with loving-kindness. You give life to the dead with great compassion. You support the fallen, heal the ill and release those bound. You fulfill Your faithfulness to those who sleep in the ground. Who is like You, Master of [all] powers, Sovereign, Who causes death and gives life and causes salvation to sprout. You are

trustworthy to give life to the dead. Blessed are You Adonai, Who gives life to the dead.

### 3. The Third Blessing: Holiness of God ("Kedushat HaShem")
You are holy, and Your name is holy, and Your holy ones will praise You every day, forever. Blessed are You Adonai the Holy God.

### 4. The Fourth Blessing: Knowledge ("Insight")
You graciously bestow knowledge to humans, and teach them understanding. Graciously bestow upon us from Yourself wisdom, understanding and knowledge. Blessed are You Adonai, Who graciously bestows knowledge.

### 5. The Fifth Blessing: Repentance ("Teshuvah")
Return us, our Father, to Your Torah and draw us near, our Sovereign, to Your service, and bring us back to complete repentance before You. Blessed are You Adonai, Who welcomes repentance.

### 6. The Sixth Blessing: Forgiveness ("Selichah")
Forgive us, our Father, for we have sinned. Pardon us, our Sovereign, for we have transgressed.  For You are a good and forgiving God. Blessed are You Adonai, gracious and forgiving.

### 7. The Seventh Blessing: Redemption ("Geulah")
Behold, please, our affliction and fight our battle, and speedily redeem us with a complete redemption, for Your name. For You God, are a mighty redeemer.  Blessed are You Adonai, Redeemer of Israel.

### 8. The Eighth Blessing: Healing ("Refuah")
Heal us, Adonai, and we will be healed. Save us and we will be saved, for You are our glory. And bring a cure and healing for all of our ailments, and all our pains, and all our wounds

for, Adonai, You are a compassionate and faithful healer. Blessed are You Adonai, Who heals God's people, Israel.

### 9. The Ninth Blessing: Economic Prosperity ("Birkat HaShanim")

Bless us, Adonai, our God, make this a blessed year and all types of its produce for good and
[In Summer:] Grant blessing [In Winter:] Grant dew and rain for blessing
upon the earth, satisfy us with its abundance and bless our year as the best of years. Blessed are You Adonai, Who blesses the years.

### 10. The Tenth Blessing: Ingathering of the Dispersed ("Kibbutz Galuyot")

Sound a great Shofar, for our freedom and raise a flag to gather our exiles, and assemble us together quickly from the four corners of the earth to our land (of Israel). Blessed are You Adonai, Who gathers the dispersed of Your people, Israel.

### 11. The Eleventh Blessing: Restoration of Justice ("Birkat HaMishpat")

Restore our Judges as in days of old, and our advisers as in the former times, and remove sorrow and anguish from our lives. Rule over us, Adonai, You alone, with loving-kindness and compassion, with righteousness and justice. Blessed are You, Adonai, Sovereign Who loves righteousness & justice.

### 12.The Twelfth Blessing: Destruction of Israel's Enemies ("Birkat HaMinim")

For the informers and the heretics, let there be no hope. Let all evil disappear in an instant. And let all Your enemies quickly be destroyed. May You quickly uproot and crush the arrogant.  May You subdue and humble them speedily in our days. Blessed are You, Adonai, Who humbles the arrogant.

### 13.The Thirteenth Blessing: Prayer for the Righteous ("Birkat HaTzadikim")

Let your tender mercies, Adonai our God, be stirred for the righteous and the pious, and on the elders of the House of Israel and its remaining scholars, and upon the righteous converts and upon us. Reward all that have true faith in Your name, and place our lot with them. May we never despair for our trust is in You. Blessed are You, Adonai, Who supports and sustains the righteous.

### 14. The Fourteenth Blessing: Restoration of Jerusalem ("Birkat Yerushalyim")

Have mercy and return to Jerusalem Your city, May your presence dwell there as You have promised. Build it now in our day and for all time. Re-establish there the majesty of David, Your servant. Blessed are You, Adonai, Who builds Jerusalem.

### 15. The Fifteenth Blessing: Coming of the Messiah ("Birkat David")

Cause the offspring of David, Your servant, to flourish and raise his horn with Your salvation, for we constantly hope for Your redemption. Blessed are You, Adonai, Who assures our redemption.

### 16. The Sixteenth Blessing: Hear our Prayer ("Tefilah")

Hear our voice Adonai our God, have pity and mercy upon us, and accept with mercy and favor our prayers, for You are God, Who hears prayers and supplications. And from before You, our Sovereign, do not turn us away unanswered for You hear the prayer of each of Your People's mouth with mercy. Blessed are You, Adonai, Who listens to prayer.

### 17. The Seventeenth Blessing: Worship ("Avodah")

Find favor, Adonai, our God, in Your people Israel, and in their prayers, and restore worship to the inner Sanctuary of Your house, and may the worship of Your people Israel always be acceptable to You. May we witness Your merciful return to Zion. Blessed are You, Adonai, Who restores the Divine Presence to Zion.

## 18. The Eighteenth Blessing: Thanksgiving ("Birkat Hoda'ah")

We are grateful to You, that You are Adonai, our God and God of our ancestors throughout all time, the Rock of our lives and Shield of our salvation for each and every generation. We will thank You and praise You for our lives that are placed in Your Hands, and for our souls, that are entrusted in Your charge, and for Your miracles that accompany us every day and for Your wonders and goodness at all times, evening, morning and afternoon. The Good [One], Your mercy never ends, The Merciful [One are You], for Your loving-kindness never ceases, We have always placed our hope in You. For all of these blessing, You are blessed, You are exalted. May every living creature praise You, God of our salvation and our assistance, the good God. Blessed are You Adonai, Who is Good, and worthy of thanks.

## 19. The Nineteenth Blessing: The Peace Blessing ("Birkat Shalom")

Grant peace in the world, good, and blessing, life, grace, kindness, and compassion upon us and upon all Israel, Your People. Bless us our Father all of us together with the light of Your countenance, For with the light of Your countenance, You gave us, Adonai, our God, Torah and life, love and kindness, righteousness and compassion, blessing and peace. And it is good in Your eyes to bless us, and to bless all Your people Israel, in every season and at all times with your gift of peace. Blessed are You Adonai, Who blesses His people of Israel with peace.

### Personal Prayer

My God, guard my tongue from evil, my lips from lies. And to those that slander me, let my soul be silent. And let my soul humble before all. Open my heart to Your Torah, and after Your mitzvot let my soul pursue. And all that plot against me, quickly nullify their schemes. Act for the sake of Your Name, act for the sake of Your compassion, Act for the sake of Your Torah, Act for the sake of Your Holiness. Answer my prayer for the deliverance of Your People. May my words and my thoughts be pleasing to You, Adonai, my Rock and my Redeemer.

May the One who makes peace on high (in the heavens), bring peace upon us and all the people Israel, And we will say, Amen.

Here are some more modern prayers that have been prayed by our Jewish brethren who continue to believe for the restoration of what God promised in His Holy Word.

### Rabbi Johnathan Sacks

O HEAVENLY ONE, Protector and Redeemer of Israel, bless the State of Israel which marks the dawning of hope for all who seek peace. Shield it beneath the wings of Your love; spread over it the canopy of Your peace; send Your light and truth to all who lead and advise, guiding them with Your good counsel. Establish peace in the land and fullness of joy for all who dwell there. Amen.

### Siddur Ashkenaz, Shabbat, Shacharit, Communal Prayers, Prayer of the State of Israel 1-35

Heavenly Father, Israel's Rock and Redeemer, bless the State of Israel, the first flowering of our redemption. Shield it under the wings of Your loving-kindness, and spread over it the Tabernacle of Your peace. Send Your light and truth to its leaders, ministers and counselors, and direct them with good counsel before You. Strengthen the hands of the defenders of our Holy Land; grant them deliverance, our God, and crown them with the crown of victory. Grant peace in the land and everlasting joy to its inhabitants. As for our brothers, the whole house of Israel, remember them in all the lands of their dispersion, and swiftly lead them upright to Zion Your city, and Jerusalem Your dwelling place, as it is written in the Torah of Moses Your servant: "Even if you are scattered to the furthermost lands under the heavens, from the Lord your God will gather you and take you back. The Lord your God will bring you to the land your ancestors possessed and you will possess it; and He will make you more prosperous and numerous than your ancestors. Then the Lord your God will open up your heart and the heart of your descendants, to love the Lord your God with all your heart and with all your soul, that you may live." (Deut. 30) Unite our hearts to love and revere Your name and observe all the words of Your Torah, and swiftly send us Your righteous anointed one of the House of David, to redeem those who long for Your salvation.

Appear in Your glorious majesty over all the dwellers on earth, and let all who breathe declare: The Lord God of Israel is King and His kingship has dominion over all. Amen, Selah.

Translation from The Koren Siddur, Rabbi Sir Jonathan Sacks (2009)


**David Seidenberg, 2018**
Our Nurturer / Our Parent, in heaven and on Earth, Rock of Israel and its redeemer, bless the State of Israel, so that she may become the beginning of the flowering of our redemption. Shield her with Your embrace of love and spread over her Your sukkah-shelter of peace, and send Your light and Your righteousness to her heads, ministers, advisers, and judges, and to the nation that elects them, and align them with the spirit of justice from You, as it says, "Zion through justice will be redeemed and her captives through righteousness." (Isaiah 1:27) Rescue all of Your land, from the Jordan River to the sea, from the spilling of blood, and all residing and sojourning there, under every

government, from haters without and hatred within. Grant peace in the land, and secure calm to her defenders, lasting joy to all her inhabitants, and real hope for all her peoples. And let us say: Amen.

*Tefilat Ha-Adam: Siddur Reformi Yisraeli L'Shabbat (2021)*

Rock and Redeemer of Yisrael, bless the State of Yisrael, the dawning of our redemption. Shield it with Your compassion and spread over it the sukkah of Your shalom. May a spark of Your spirit inspire the actions of its elected leaders and officials, judges and advisors that they may follow the path of justice, liberty and righteousness. Strengthen the spirit and the hands of those who build and protect our holy land and grant them salvation and life. Bring shalom to this land and everlasting joy to its inhabitants. Be with all the people of Israel wherever they are. Plant within their hearts the love of Zion, and may those of our people who are so inspired, come to Jerusalem, Your city, which bears Your name. Spread Your spirit over all the inhabitants of our land. Uproot hatred and animosity, jealousy and evil. Plant in our hearts love and kinship, peace and friendship. And speedily fulfill the vision of Your prophet: Nation will not lift up sword against nation, neither shall they learn war anymore. And let us say: Amen

If you call yourself a Believer in Yeshua-Jesus, I encourage you to join with me in praying for the Jewish people and the Land of Israel.

**Psalm 122:6-9** (TLV) Pray for the peace of Jerusalem— "May those who love you be at peace! 7 May there be *shalom* within your walls— quietness within your palaces." 8 For the sake of my brothers and friends, I now say: "*Shalom* be within you." 9 For the sake of the House of *Adonai* our God, I will seek your good.

Pray for the peace, prosperity and protection of Jerusalem and the Land of Israel. Pray for every hostage to be returned and the Land of Israel no longer occupied by the spirit of violence. Pray that the fullness of the nations to come to Messiah and they learn and walk in His Kingdom Ways. Pray that all Israel will be saved and come to the knowledge of their Messiah Yeshua.

Pray for the blindness, stubbornness, and stumbling blocks of Israel to be removed. Pray that they see Yeshua, the One pierced for them. Pray they return with heartfelt repentance and embrace their Messianic King.

Pray the promises, pray the Word, and remind God of His Word and Covenant as you pray. According to Isaiah 43:26, put God in remembrance and remind Him so you can plead and be in agreement with Him.

Use these Scriptures as a reference and reminder for you and to pray back to the Lord concerning His Land and beloved people. I hope you have found this book both timely, insightful, and as a reference in the biblical mandate to pray and stand with Israel and the Jewish people until every one of these promises are completely fulfilled and lived. All for the glory and praise to Yeshua, our Messiah and King of Israel.

## Scriptures that affirm the Land of Israel and the Jewish People

**Genesis 15:18-21** (TLV) On that day Adonai cut a covenant with Abram, saying, "I give this land to your seed, from the river of Egypt to the great river, the Euphrates River: 19 the Kenite, the Kenizzites, the Kadmonites, 20 the Hittites, the

Perizzites, the Raphaites, 21 the Amorites, the Canaanites, the Girgashites, and the Jebusites."

**Genesis 28:10-15** AMP Now Jacob left Beersheba [never to see his mother again] and traveled toward Haran. 11 And he came to a certain place and stayed overnight there because the sun had set. Taking one of the stones of the place, he put it under his head and lay down there [to sleep]. 12 He dreamed that there was a ladder (stairway) placed on the earth, and the top of it reached [out of sight] toward heaven; and [he saw] the angels of God ascending and descending on it [going to and from heaven]. 13 And behold, the Lord stood above and around him and said, "I am the Lord, the God of Abraham your [father's] father and the God of Isaac; I will give to you and to your descendants the land [of promise] on which you are lying. 14 Your descendants shall be as [countless as] the dust of the earth, and you shall spread abroad to the west and the east and the north and the south; and all the families (nations) of the earth shall be blessed through you and your descendants. 15 Behold, I am with you and will keep [careful watch over you and guard] you wherever you may go, and I will bring you back to this [promised] land; for I will not leave you until I have done what I have promised you."

**Deuteronomy 30:5** (AMP) The Lord your God will bring you into the land which your fathers possessed, and you will take possession of it; and He shall make you prosper and multiply—even more than your fathers.

**Isaiah 11:11-12** (AMP) Then it will happen on that day that the Lord will again acquire with His hand a second time the remnant of His people, who will remain, from Assyria, from [Lower] Egypt, from Pathros, from Cush (Ethiopia), from Elam [in Persia], from Shinar [Babylonia], from Hamath [in Aram], And from the coastlands bordering the [Mediterranean] Sea. 12 And He will lift up a signal for the nations and assemble the outcasts of Israel, and will gather the dispersed of Judah from the four corners of the earth.

**Jeremiah 23:3-8** (AMP) "Then I will gather the remnant of My flock out of all the countries to which I have driven them and bring them back to their folds and pastures; and they will be fruitful and multiply. 4 I will set up shepherds over them who will feed them. And they will not be afraid any longer, nor be terrified, nor will any be missing," says the Lord. 5 "Behold (listen closely), the days are coming," says the Lord, "When I will raise up for David a righteous Branch; And He will reign as King and act wisely and will do [those things that accomplish] justice and righteousness in the land. 6 "In His days Judah will be saved, And Israel will dwell safely; Now this is His name by which He will be called; 'The Lord Our Righteousness.' 7 "Therefore behold, the days are coming," says the Lord, "when they will no longer say, 'As the Lord lives, who brought up the children of Israel from the land of Egypt,' 8 but [they will say], 'As the Lord lives, who brought up and led back the descendants of the house of Israel from the north country and from all the countries to which I had driven them.' Then they will live in their own land."

**Ezekiel 37:21-25** AMP Say to them, 'Thus says the Lord God, "Behold, I am going to take the children of Israel from among the nations where they have gone, and I will gather them from every side and bring them into their own land; 22 and I will make them one nation in the land, on the mountains of Israel; and one king will be king over all of them; and they will no longer be two nations, and will no longer be divided into two kingdoms. 23 They will no longer defile themselves with their idols, or with their detestable things, or with any of their transgressions; but I will save them from all their transgressions in which they have sinned, and I will cleanse them. So they will be My people, and I will be their God. 24 "My servant David will be king over them, and they all will have one shepherd. They will also walk in

My ordinances and keep My statutes and observe them. 25 They will live in the land where your fathers lived, [the land] that I gave to My servant Jacob, and they will live there, they and their children and their children's children, forever; and My servant David will be their leader forever.

**Isaiah 60:18-21** (AMP) "Violence will not be heard again in your land, nor devastation or destruction within your borders; but you will call your walls Salvation, and your gates Praise [to God]. 19 "The sun will no longer be your light by day, nor shall the bright glow of the moon give light to you, but the Lord will be an everlasting light for you; and your God will be your glory and splendor. 20 "Your sun will no longer set, nor will your moon wane; for the Lord will be your everlasting light, and the days of your mourning will be over. 21 "Then all your people will be [uncompromisingly and consistently] righteous; they will possess the land forever, the branch of My planting, the work of My hands, that I may be glorified.

**Jeremiah 24:5-6** (AMP) "Thus says the Lord, the God of Israel, 'Like these good figs, so I will regard as good the captives of Judah, whom I have sent from this place into the land of the Chaldeans. 6 For I will set My eyes on them for good, and I will bring them again to this land; and I will build them up and not overwhelm them, and I will plant them and not uproot them.

**Jeremiah 30:18** (AMP) "Thus says the Lord, 'Behold (hear this), I will restore the fortunes of the tents of Jacob and have mercy on his dwelling places; The city will be rebuilt on its [old, mound-like] ruin, And the palace will stand on its rightful place.

**Jeremiah 31:31-34** (AMP) "Behold, the days are coming," says the Lord, "when I will make a new covenant with the house of Israel (the Northern Kingdom) and with the house of Judah (the Southern Kingdom), 32 not like the covenant which I made with their fathers in the day when I took them by the hand to bring them out of the land of Egypt, My covenant which they broke, although I was a husband to them," says the Lord. 33 "But this is the covenant which I will make with the house of Israel after those days," says the Lord, "I will put My law within them, and I will write it on their hearts; and I will be their God, and they will be My people. 34 And each man will no longer teach his neighbor and his brother, saying, 'Know the Lord,' for they will all know Me [through personal experience], from the least of them to the greatest," says the Lord. "For I will forgive their wickedness, and I will no longer remember their sin."

**Jeremiah 32:37-40** (AMP) Behold, I will gather them out of all countries to which I have driven them in My anger, in My wrath and in great indignation; and I will bring them back to this place and make them live in safety. 38 They will be My people, and I will be their God; 39 and I will give them one heart and one way, that they may [reverently] fear Me forever, for their own good and for the good of their children after them. 40 I will make an everlasting covenant with them that I will do them good and not turn away from them; and I will put in their heart a fear and reverential awe of Me, so that they will not turn away from Me.

**Jeremiah 33:6-9** (AMP) Behold, [in the restored Jerusalem] I will bring to it health and healing, and I will heal them; and I will reveal to them an abundance of peace (prosperity, security, stability) and truth. 7 I will restore the fortunes of Judah and the fortunes of Israel and will rebuild them as they were at first. 8 I will cleanse them from all their wickedness (guilt) by which they have sinned against Me, and I will pardon (forgive) all their sins by which they rebelled against Me. 9 Jerusalem will be to Me a name of joy, praise and glory before all the nations of the earth which will hear of all the good that I do for it, and they shall fear and tremble because of all the good and all the peace (prosperity, security, stability) that I provide for it.'

**Ezekiel 28:25-26** (AMP) 'Thus says the Lord God, "When I gather the house of Israel from the nations among whom they are scattered, and I manifest my Holiness in them in the sight of the nations, then they will live in their own land which I gave to My servant Jacob. 26 They shall live in it securely; and they will build houses, plant vineyards and live securely when I execute judgment on all those around them who despise them. Then they will know [with clarity and confidence] that I am the Lord their God."'"

**Ezekiel 34:11-12** (AMP) For thus says the Lord God, "Behold, I Myself will search for My flock and seek them out. 12 As a shepherd cares for his sheep on the day that he is among his scattered flock, so I will care for My sheep; and I will rescue them from all the places to which they were scattered on a cloudy and gloomy day.

**Ezekiel 34:24-26** (AMP) And I the Lord will be their God, and My servant David will be a prince among them; I the Lord have spoken. 25 "I will make a covenant of peace with them and will eliminate the predatory animals from the land so that they may live securely in the wilderness and sleep [safely] in the woods. 26 I will make them and the places around My hill (Jerusalem, Zion) a blessing. And I will make showers come down in their season; there will be [abundant] showers of blessing (divine favor).

**Ezekiel 39:29** (AMP) I will not hide My face from them any longer, because I will have poured out My Spirit on the house of Israel," says the Lord God.

**Hosea 3:4-5** (AMP) For the sons of Israel will remain for many days without king or prince, without sacrifice or [idolatrous] pillar, and without ephod or teraphim (household idols). 5 Afterward the sons of Israel will return [in deep repentance] and seek the Lord their God and [seek from the line of] David their king [the King of kings—the Messiah];

and they will come trembling to the Lord and to His goodness and blessing in the last days.

**Joel 2:18-27** (AMP) Then the Lord will be jealous for His land [ready to defend it since it is rightfully and uniquely His] And will have compassion on His people [and will spare them]. 19 The Lord will answer and say to His people, "Behold, I am going to send you grain and new wine and oil, and you will be satisfied in full with them; And I will never again make you an object of ridicule among the [Gentile] nations. 20 "But I will remove the northern army far away from you, And I will drive it into a parched and desolate land, With its forward guard into the eastern sea (Dead Sea) And with its rear guard into the western sea (Mediterranean Sea). And its stench will arise and its foul odor of decay will come up [this is the fate of the northern army in the final day of the Lord], For He has done great things." 21 Do not fear, O land; be glad and rejoice, For the Lord has done great things! 22 Do not be afraid, you animals of the field, For the pastures of the wilderness have turned green; The tree has produced its fruit, And the fig tree and the vine have yielded in full. 23 So rejoice, O children of Zion, And delight in the Lord, your God; For He has given you the early [autumn] rain in vindication And He has poured down the rain for you, The early [autumn] rain and the late [spring] rain, as before. 24 And the threshing floors shall be full of grain, And the vats shall overflow with new wine and oil. 25 "And I will compensate you for the years That the swarming locust has eaten, the creeping locust, the stripping locust, and the gnawing locust— My great army which I sent among you. 26 "You will have plenty to eat and be satisfied And praise the name of the Lord your God Who has dealt wondrously with you; And My people shall never be put to shame.
27 "And you shall know [without any doubt] that I am in the midst of Israel [to protect and bless you], And that I am the Lord your God, and there is no other; My people will never be put to shame.

**Amos 9:14-15** AMP "Also I shall bring back the exiles of My people Israel, and they will rebuild the deserted *and* ruined cities and inhabit them: They will also plant vineyards and drink their wine, and make gardens and eat their fruit. 15 "I will also plant them on their land, and they shall never again be uprooted from their land Which I have given them," Says the Lord your God.

**Micah 2:12** (AMP) "I shall most certainly assemble all of you, O Jacob; I shall surely gather the remnant of Israel. I shall bring them together like sheep in the fold [multiplying the nation]; Like a flock in the midst of its pasture. The place will swarm with many people *and* hum loudly with noise.

**Micah 4:6-7** (AMP) "In that day," says the Lord, "I shall assemble the lame, and gather the outcasts [from foreign captivity], Even those whom I have caused pain. 7"I shall make the lame a [godly] remnant and the outcasts a strong nation; And the Lord shall reign over them in Mount Zion from this time on and forever.

**Zephaniah 3:19-20** (AMP) "Behold, at that time I am going to deal with all your oppressors; I will save the lame and gather the scattered, and I will turn their shame into praise and renown in every land [where they have suffered]. 20 "At that time I will bring you in, yes, at the time I gather you together; for I will make you a name and a praise among all the peoples of the earth when I restore your fortunes [and freedom] before your eyes,"
says the Lord.

**Zechariah 8:7-8** (AMP) Thus says the Lord of hosts, 'Behold, I am going to save My people from the east country and from the west, 8 and I will bring them home and they will live in the midst of Jerusalem; and they shall be My people, and I will be their God in truth (faithfulness) and in righteousness.'

**Zechariah 13:8-9** (AMP) "It will come about in all the land," Declares the Lord, "Two parts in it will be cut off and perish, But the third will be left alive. 9 "And I will bring the third part through the fire, refine them as silver is refined, and test them as gold is tested. They will call on My name, And I will listen and answer them; I will say, 'They are My people,' And they will say, 'The Lord is my God.'"

**Isaiah 51:1-3** (AMP) "Listen to Me, you who pursue righteousness (right standing with God), Who seek and inquire of the Lord: Look to the rock from which you were cut and to the excavation of the quarry from which you were dug. 2 "Look to Abraham your father and to Sarah who gave birth to you in pain; For I called him when he was but one, Then I blessed him and made him many." 3 For the Lord will comfort Zion [in her captivity]; He will comfort all her ruins. And He will make her wilderness like Eden, and her desert like the garden of the Lord; Joy and gladness will be found in her, Thanksgiving and the voice of a melody.

**Isaiah 61:1-7** (AMP) The Spirit of the Lord God is upon me, Because the Lord has anointed and commissioned me To bring good news to the humble and afflicted; He has sent me to bind up [the wounds of] the brokenhearted, To proclaim release [from confinement and condemnation] to the [physical and spiritual] captives And freedom to prisoners, 2 To proclaim the favorable year of the Lord, And the day of vengeance and retribution of our God, To comfort all who mourn, 3 To grant to those who mourn in Zion the following: To give them a turban instead of dust [on their heads, a sign of mourning], The oil of joy instead of mourning, The garment [expressive] of praise instead of a disheartened spirit. So they will be called the trees of righteousness [strong and magnificent, distinguished for integrity, justice, and right standing with God], The planting of the Lord, that He may be glorified. 4 Then they will rebuild the ancient ruins, they will raise up and restore the former desolations; And they will renew the ruined cities, The

desolations (deserted settlements) of many generations.
5 Strangers will stand and feed your flocks, and foreigners will be your farmers and your vinedressers. 6 But you shall be called the priests of the Lord; People will speak of you as the ministers of our God. You will eat the wealth of nations, and you will boast of their riches. 7 Instead of your [former] shame you will have a double portion; And instead of humiliation your people will shout for joy over their portion. Therefore in their land they will possess double [what they had forfeited]; Everlasting joy will be theirs.

**Isaiah 66:7-13** (AMP) "Before she (Zion) was in labor, she gave birth; Before her labor pain came, she gave birth to a boy. 8 "Who has heard of such a thing? Who has seen such things? Can a land be born in one day? Or can a nation be brought forth in a moment? As soon as Zion was in labor, she also brought forth her sons. 9 "Shall I bring to the moment of birth and not give delivery?" says the Lord. "Or shall I who gives delivery shut *the womb*?" says your God. 10 "Rejoice with Jerusalem and be glad for her, all you who love her; Rejoice greatly with her, all you who mourn over her, 11 That you may nurse and be satisfied with her comforting breasts, That you may drink deeply and be delighted with her bountiful bosom." 12 For the Lord says this, "Behold, I extend peace to her (Jerusalem) like a river, And the glory of the nations like an overflowing stream; And you will be nursed, you will be carried on *her* hip and [playfully] rocked on *her* knees. 13 "As one whom his mother comforts, so I will comfort you; And you will be comforted in Jerusalem."

**Zechariah 12:6-10** (AMP) "In that day I will make the clans of Judah like a firepot in a woodpile, and like a flaming torch among sheaves [of grain]. They will devour all the surrounding peoples on the right hand and on the left; and the people of Jerusalem will again live [securely] in their own place, in Jerusalem. 7 The Lord shall save the tents of Judah first, so that the glory of the house of David and the glory of the inhabitants of Jerusalem will not be magnified above Judah. 8 In that day the Lord will defend the people of Jerusalem, and the one who is impaired among them in that day [of persecution] will become [strong and noble] like David; and the house of David will be like God, like the Angel of the Lord [who is] before them. 9 And in that day I will seek to destroy all the nations that come against Jerusalem. 10 "I will pour out on the house of David and on the people of Jerusalem, the Spirit of grace (unmerited favor) and supplication. And they will look at Me whom they have pierced; and they will mourn for Him as one mourns for an only son, and they will weep bitterly over Him as one who weeps bitterly over a firstborn.

**Romans 11:1-3** (AMP) I say then, has God rejected and disowned His people? Certainly not! For I too am an Israelite, a descendant of Abraham, of the tribe of Benjamin. 2 God has not rejected His [chosen] people whom He foreknew. Or do you not know what the Scripture says of Elijah, how he pleads with God against Israel? 3 "Lord, they have killed Your prophets, they have torn down Your altars, and I alone am left [of the prophets], and they are seeking my life."

**Romans 11:25-27** (TLV) For I do not want you, brothers and sisters, to be ignorant of this mystery—lest you be wise in your own eyes—that a partial hardening has come upon Israel until the fullness of the Gentiles has come in; 26 and in this way all Israel will be saved, as it is written, "The Deliverer shall come out of Zion. He shall turn away ungodliness from Jacob. 27 And this is My covenant with them, when I take away their sins."

# Chapter 7

## Group or Personal Study

1. Write down some of your own personal prayer points to pray for the Jewish people and the Land of Israel.

_____
_____
_____
_____
_____

2. What are some of your favorite Scriptures on prayer?

_____
_____
_____
_____
_____

3. Now use those favorite passages and begin to use them as a starting point in your prayers for the Jewish people and the Land of Israel.

_____
_____
_____
_____
_____

4. Do a search and find scriptures that have to do with God answering prayers. These promises will be a foundation to build your faith on when praying.

_____
_____
_____
_____
_____

5. List some of those Scriptures you have found or put them in a "note" as a resource for your prayer time.

_____
_____
_____
_____
_____

6. Have you ever thought about praying three times a day? What would be the benefits? What would be some of your greatest challenges to do that?

_____
_____
_____
_____
_____

7. Since what we call the Lord's Prayer is actually a "disciple's prayer guide," how can you use it as a template to pray for Israel and the Jewish people?

_____
_____
_____
_____
_____

8. Make a list of some of the prayers God has already answered for you. Thank Him for what He did for you in the past, for they testify to God's mercy, grace, and love.

_____
_____
_____
_____
_____

9. If you are in a small group, commit to praying for Israel every time you gather. If you're reading this for your own personal growth, commit to pray for the Jewish people and the Land of Israel daily. Begin Now!

_____

_____

_____

_____

_____

**Psalm 122:6-9** (TLV)
Pray for the peace of Jerusalem—
"May those who love you be at peace! 7 May there be _shalom_ within your walls— quietness within your palaces." 8 For the sake of my brothers and friends, I now say: "_Shalom_ be within you." 9 For the sake of the House of _Adonai_ our God, I will seek your good.

# BOOKS BY KENNETH S. ALBIN

YOU ARE BORN FOR GREATNESS

YOU ARE BORN FOR THE EXTRAORDINARY

UPSIDE OF DOWN ( Spanish, Portuguese, Russian)

THE MYSTERY OF THE CROWN

HACKED: THE HEBREW CHRISTIAN( Spanish, Portuguese, Russian)

CHRISTIANS GET TO CELEBRATE PASSOVER TOO!

NO MORE LEAVEN

HIT THE MARK

HIDDEN BLESSINGS REVEALED

TABERNACLES IT'S A CELEBRATION & NOT JUST AN OPTION!

HANUKKAH AND PURIM ARE FOR CHRISTIANS TOO

THE BLESSINGS OF PENTECOST

THE HEBREW CHRISTIAN LIFE

THE BLESSING OF ABRAHAM (Spanish, Portuguese)

SUPERNATURAL DISCIPLESHIP ( Portuguese)

MY DAILY TORAH READING PLAN & DEVOTIONAL (SERIES)

Contact Information: for Ken Albin
www.savethenations.com / www.hitthemarktorah.tv


**Bio:** Kenny Albin called by his Jewish mother always believed he would be a "Rabbi. For over 30 years as a born again jewish christian pastor Kenneth was awakened to walk in the Torah way of His Messiah.He now teaches this Torah Way to all through Save the Nations based presently in South Florida but has influence in Israel, Brazil and many Nations of the world. His mom's prayers have finally been answered!

# BOOKS BY KENNETH S. ALBIN

YOU ARE BORN FOR GREATNESS

YOU ARE BORN FOR THE EXTRAORDINARY

UPSIDE OF DOWN ( Spanish, Portuguese, Russian)

THE MYSTERY OF THE CROWN

HACKED: THE HEBREW CHRISTIAN( Spanish, Portuguese, Russian)

CHRISTIANS GET TO CELEBRATE PASSOVER TOO!

NO MORE LEAVEN

HIT THE MARK

HIDDEN BLESSINGS REVEALED

TABERNACLES IT'S A CELEBRATION & NOT JUST AN OPTION!

HANUKKAH AND PURIM ARE FOR CHRISTIANS TOO

THE BLESSINGS OF PENTECOST

THE HEBREW CHRISTIAN LIFE

THE BLESSING OF ABRAHAM (Spanish, Portuguese)

SUPERNATURAL DISCIPLESHIP ( Portuguese)

MY DAILY TORAH READING PLAN & DEVOTIONAL (English and Spanish Series)

Contact Information: for Ken Albin
www.savethenations.com / www.hitthemarktorah.tv


Bio: Kenny Albin called by his jewish mother always believed he would be a "Rabbi. For over 30 years as a born again jewish christian pastor Kenneth was awakened to walk in the Torah way of His Messiah.He now teaches this Torah Way to all through Save the Nations based presently in South Florida but has influence in Israel, Brazil and many Nations of the world. His mom's prayers have finally been answered!

www.ingramcontent.com/pod-product-compliance
Lightning Source LLC
Chambersburg PA
CBHW060202100426
42744CB00007B/1130